my **revision** notes

OCR GCSE (9–1)

BUSINESS

Mike Schofield

HODDER EDUCATION
AN HACHETTE UK COMPANY

Although every effort has been made to ensure that website addresses are correct at time of going to press, Hodder Education cannot be held responsible for the content of any website mentioned in this book. It is sometimes possible to find a relocated web page by typing in the address of the home page for a website in the URL window of your browser.

Hachette UK's policy is to use papers that are natural, renewable and recyclable products and made from wood grown in sustainable forests. The logging and manufacturing processes are expected to conform to the environmental regulations of the country of origin.

Orders: please contact Bookpoint Ltd, 130 Park Drive, Milton Park, Abingdon, Oxon OX14 4SE. Telephone: +44 (0)1235 827827. Fax: +44 (0)1235 400401. Email education@bookpoint.co.uk Lines are open from 9 a.m. to 5 p.m., Monday to Saturday, with a 24-hour message answering service. You can also order through our website: www.hoddereducation.co.uk

ISBN: 978 1 5104 2369 5

© Mike Schofield 2018

First published by Pearson Education Limited
Published from 2018 by Hodder Education,
An Hachette UK Company
Carmelite House
50 Victoria Embankment
London EC4Y 0DZ

www.hoddereducation.co.uk

Impression number 10 9 8 7 6 5 4 3 2 1
Year 2022 2021 2020 2019 2018

All rights reserved. Apart from any use permitted under UK copyright law, no part of this publication may be reproduced or transmitted in any form or by any means, electronic or mechanical, including photocopying and recording, or held within any information storage and retrieval system, without permission in writing from the publisher or under licence from the Copyright Licensing Agency Limited. Further details of such licences (for reprographic reproduction) may be obtained from the Copyright Licensing Agency Limited, www.cla.co.uk

Cover photo © Rawpixel.com/Shutterstock

Illustrations by Integra Software Services Pvt. Ltd, Pondicherry, India

Typeset by Integra Software Services Pvt. Ltd, Pondicherry, India

Printed in Spain by Graphycems

A catalogue record for this title is available from the British Library.

Get the most from this book

Everyone has to decide his or her own revision strategy, but it is essential to review your work, learn it and test your understanding. When you revise, be active. Use a pen. Most people do not remember everything simply by reading. Make notes, use key words and lists, draw diagrams and pictures and use Post-it notes – whatever works for you.

These Revision Notes will help you to revise in a planned way, topic by topic. Use this book as the cornerstone of your revision and don't hesitate to write in it – personalise your notes and check your progress by ticking off each section as you revise. The book has been written so that, whenever possible, a single page covers one bullet point from one topic in the specification. Learning points are summarised using diagrams or tables or short texts. You are advised to work through each page in order.

Tick to track your progress

Use the revision planner on pages 4–5 to plan your revision, topic by topic. Tick the boxes for each topic when you have revised it, tested it using the Now test yourself feature and the online answers and when you have ticked off all the 'I can' tasks in the topic checklist.

My revision planner

REVISED TESTED EXAM READY

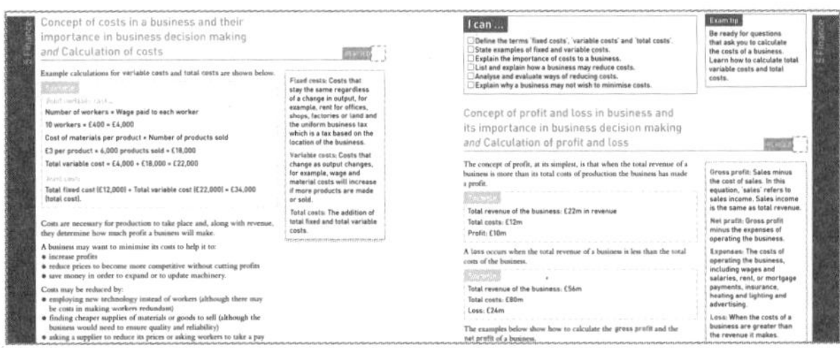

Features to help you succeed

Exam tips

Expert tips are given throughout the book to help you polish your exam technique in order to maximise your chances in the exam.

Key terms

Clear, concise definitions of essential key terms are provided where they first appear. Learn these terms.

Now test yourself

Questions, both multiple choice and case study questions, are given throughout the book. Practise answering these. For case study questions, you can write bullet points or a full answer.

'I can' checklist

Read through the 'I can' statements. Only tick each item you are confident with. Unticked items will guide your further revision.

Online

Go online to check your answers to the Now test yourself questions at **www.hoddereducation.co.uk/myrevisionnotesdownloads**

Remember that there is often more than one possible answer for a question.

My revision planner

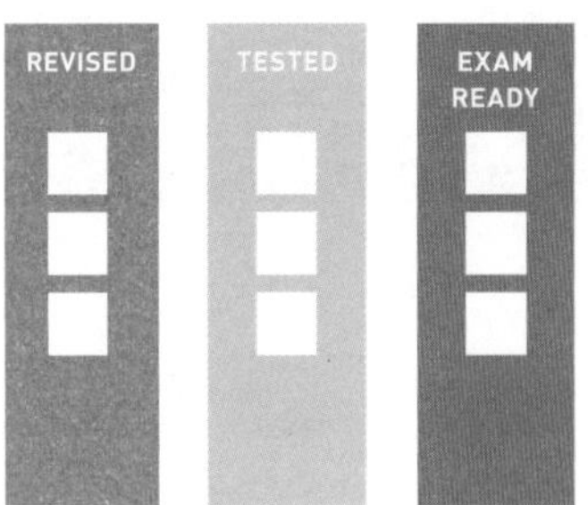

Now test yourself answers at
www.hoddereducation.co.uk/myrevisionnotesdownloads

Countdown to my exams

10–3 weeks before the examination – Revision 1

- Be active when revising – make notes, summarise key words, draw diagrams.
- Answer the 'Now test yourself' questions and compare with online answers.
- Read the 'Exam tips' and tick off the 'I can checklist'.
- After each page has been revised, record your progress in the 'My revision planner' on pages 4–5.
- Aim to cover *one* section of the specification each week. You are advised to study the sections in order. Once you have covered Sections 1 to 3, you will have learnt all you need to know for the first examination – Business 1. Test yourself by looking at the specimen paper for Business 1. The papers and mark schemes are available from the OCR website (**www.ocr.org.uk**). Business 2 covers Sections 4 to 7, so use a similar approach for these topics.
- Remember to include any revision classes put on by your teacher in your plan. Your teacher will be a great help in preparing you to answer questions in the examination.

REVISED ☐

2–1 week before the examination – Revision 2

- Use the 'My revision planner' page for Revision 2. Focus on those areas where you were not confident enough to tick the 'I can' statements.
- Revise Sections 1 to 3 in the first week and Sections 4 to 7 in the second week. Test yourself using a different past paper and mark scheme.

REVISED ☐

Final week

- Look at one more Business 1 paper and one more Business 2 paper or questions from the Hodder textbook *OCR GCSE (9–1) Business*.
- Revise again those areas you do not feel totally confident about.

REVISED ☐

The day before the examination

- Check the time and place of your examination.
- Make sure you have everything you will need – a pen and a couple of spares, pencil, rubber, ruler, watch, tissues, a bottle of water and maybe some sweets.
- Have one last look over any area of the specification that you are still not totally confident about.
- Allow some time to relax and have an early night to ensure you are fresh and alert for the examinations.

REVISED ☐

In the examination

- Read the questions and the case studies carefully – twice is a good idea. Make sure you know what the questions are asking you to do.
- Divide your time up. A useful guide is 15 minutes for the 15 multiple choice questions and 25 minutes for each of the case study questions.
- Make sure you answer ALL the questions – you will throw marks away if you do not provide any answer, even if you are not confident about what you have written, you have some chance of picking up some marks.
- Don't panic. If you have done your revision, you should be able to answer every question. Think about the type of questions, for example, if it is an evaluation question, think about the evaluation strategies you have learnt.

REVISED ☐

My exams

Business 1

Date: ....

Time: ....

Location: ....

Business 2

Date: ....

Time: ....

Location: ....

1 Business activity

1.1 Role of business enterprise and entrepreneurship

Purpose of business enterprise and entrepreneurship

REVISED

Figure 1.1 shows the three main purposes of business enterprise and entrepreneurship. An **entrepreneur** may see an existing product and **spot an opportunity** to develop and improve it.

Three purposes of business enterprise and entrepreneurship

Spotting an opportunity
- Spotting a gap in the market
- Improving a product or service already provided
- Producing a product or service more cheaply

Developing an idea
- Designing the product or service
- Planning production

Satisfying customer needs
- Producing the product or providing the service
- Marketing the product or service

Figure 1.1 Main purposes of business enterprise and entrepreneurship

Now test yourself

TESTED

The entrepreneurs that developed Spotify saw an opportunity: ICT could be used to sell and deliver music, podcasts and video streaming. The consumer can buy the product online in the comfort of their own home and receive immediate delivery. The entrepreneurs worked with record labels and independent musicians to sell their music in return for a royalty. They then put in place the technology to enable this to work, such as the software to be able to stream the content to buyers and to take payment from them. Spotify sells directly to the consumer and so distribution costs as well as the cost of managing shops is saved. Spotify customers say the service is much better than going to shops to buy music.

Analyse **two** ways in which Spotify satisfies consumer needs. [6]

Entrepreneur: A person who takes the risk of starting and running a business enterprise.

Spotting an opportunity: The ability to see the need for a particular product or service customers need.

Exam tip

When answering 'analyse' questions, always apply your answer to the business in the case study. For example, when answering the 'Now test yourself' about satisfying customer needs, stress that Spotify has met the need by offering a faster service at a lower cost. Explain why Spotify has been able to do this.

I can ...

- ☐ State three purposes of business enterprise and entrepreneurs.
- ☐ Analyse examples of businesses spotting opportunities and developing ideas.

Characteristics of an entrepreneur

REVISED

'Characteristics' refers to the qualities, skills or abilities that a person must have to be a successful entrepreneur. There are four main **characteristics of entrepreneurs**, as shown in Figure 1.2.

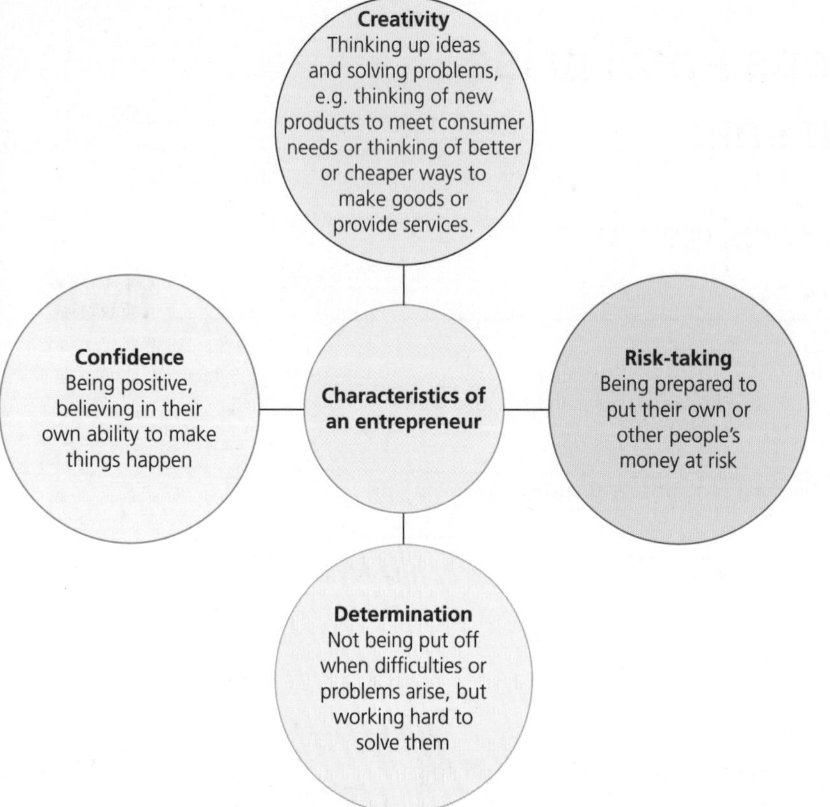

Figure 1.2 Characteristics of an entrepreneur

Characteristics of an entrepreneur: The features of an entrepreneur, which include being determined, creative and having the ability and confidence to take risks.

I can ...

- ☐ State and explain four characteristics that an entrepreneur should have.
- ☐ Analyse the characteristics of an entrepreneur in the context of a case study.

Exam tip

In the examination carefully read the case study. Think about how the information in it matches what you have learnt and revised; in this case, how the characteristics of entrepreneurs were demonstrated by James Dyson. Then explain how these characteristics helped him to make a success of his business.

Now test yourself

TESTED

Frustrated by a poor-quality vacuum cleaner which he used in his home, James Dyson created the idea of the bagless vacuum cleaner. Dyson gave up his paid job and used his savings while he worked in his garage to produce something better. Showing great determination, he tried out of over 500 different designs, believing that, in the end, he would be successful. During this time, his wife worked as a teacher to support them. Dyson then risked his money to start up a business producing and selling the vacuum cleaners.

Analyse **two** characteristics of an entrepreneur that helped James Dyson to succeed when starting up his business. [6]

Risks and rewards of being an entrepreneur

REVISED

Entrepreneurs hope for **rewards** when they go into business, but they are taking **risks** by doing this. These are summarised in Table 1.1.

Table 1.1 Risks and rewards of entrepreneurship

	Risks	Rewards
Financial	• If the business does not succeed, the risk of losing savings (and other assets) to pay off debts.	• The potential to make a lot of money.
Non-financial	• Health – the strain of running a business can cause mental and physical illness.	• Independence – being in control of what you do; not being told what to do by others. • Self-satisfaction – feeling good because the business is a success. • Making a difference – improving the lives of customers; providing socially responsible goods and services.

Now test yourself

TESTED

1 Which of the following is **not** a risk of being an entrepreneur? [1]
 (a) Making a loss
 (b) Feeling satisfied about making a success of starting a business
 (c) Experiencing poor health
 (d) Suffering from strained relationships with friends and family

2 Amelia Prendergast bought a small newsagent shop using her own savings and a loan from a bank. She had been fed up in her office work as an accounts clerk and wanted to run her own business. She really struggled having to get up at 5 a.m. each day, sorting the papers in to 'rounds' for the paper boys and girls to deliver and then working in the shop all day until she closed at 6 p.m. After three months, exhausted and stressed, Amelia put the shop up for sale. However, in the time that she ran the business, she had increased the number of customers and the revenue the shop earned. Amelia sold the business for more than she had paid for it.

 Evaluate the risks and rewards to Amelia of being an entrepreneur. [9]

Rewards: The benefits an entrepreneur receives from starting up and running a business. They may be financial or non-financial.

Risks: The possible losses that an entrepreneur may suffer from starting up and running a business.

Exam tip

When evaluating the risks and rewards of being an entrepreneur, write about the rewards the person has gained as well as the risks they have faced and what it has cost them. Remember to use the evidence in the case study so that you are applying your learning. Always make a judgement – have the risks and rewards been worthwhile or not? Sometimes you may want to suggest further information that would help you make your conclusion.

I can ...

- ☐ State two risks that entrepreneurs may take.
- ☐ State four rewards that entrepreneurs may receive.
- ☐ Evaluate whether an entrepreneur is receiving sufficient reward for the risks he or she is taking.

1.2 Business planning

Purpose of planning business activity

REVISED

A business must plan its activities to:

- reduce the risk of failure – for example, it must think about the prices and goods competitors offer
- be as successful as possible – for example, decide the kind of people it needs to run the business and how to market its product as effectively as possible.

Figure 1.3 shows the steps involved in developing a business idea.

Figure 1.3 Steps involved in developing a business idea

Aims and objectives: Statements of what the business is trying to achieve, such as grow larger or make a profit.

Business plan: A simple plan which sets out details of the product or service being sold and how it will be financed, marketed and details of market research findings.

Finance: A business word used instead of money. The finance needed to start a business is the money required to buy the resources needed.

Markets: Where a business sells its goods or services.

Resources: The things a business needs to make it work, including staff and materials.

Now test yourself

TESTED

A case study was produced by www.englandgolf.org. The focus of the study was Dunning Golf Club, which had produced a plan about how it should increase its membership and profitability. The plan included the following:

- improving the golf course
- offering more benefits to paid-up members (such as subsidised lessons)
- using outside caterers to ensure better and cheaper catering
- more clearly stated priorities for the future and how these would be financed.

Explain the purpose of writing a business plan, such as that produced by Dunning Golf Club. [4]

I can ...

- [ ] Explain the main purposes of a business plan.

Role, importance and usefulness of a business plan

REVISED

A business plan explains how a business intends to achieve its objectives. It may be written before the business starts, or when planning a major change to the way an existing business **operates**.

A good business plan will cover all the objectives shown in Figure 1.4. It will also make these objectives SMART:

- **S**pecific – clearly stating what is to be achieved.
- **M**easureable – stating how to measure the **success** of the plan using, for example, sales or profits.
- **A**chievable – the targets are possible for the business to achieve.
- **R**ealistic – the targets are appropriate for the business.
- **T**imely – the plan includes a deadline for achieving the targets.

Operate: A term used to explain how a business works.

Success: For a business, success can take many forms, including making a profit, surviving and providing a good service to customers.

Identifying the market, for example, the age, gender and income of target customers.

Identifying the resources needed to operate the business, for example, workers, type of equipment or machinery to be used.

Business plan

Identify the finance needed to start up or grow the business and how this will be achieved, for example, selling shares, obtaining a loan or overdraft.

Achieve the business' aims and objectives, for example, making a profit, expected sales, achieving social objectives.

Figure 1.4 A business plan details how a business intends to achieve its objectives

Exam tip

When evaluating a business plan, write about what it contains and what other information might be useful. Does it cover all four areas identified in the business plan diagram? Is it SMART – does it give measureable and timed targets?

Now test yourself

TESTED

1 A business plan is useful because it will: [1]
  (a) make sure a business cannot fail.
  (b) help competitors to improve.
  (c) identify the resources that a business needs to succeed
  (d) reduce the costs of running the business.
2 Using the information provided on page 10, evaluate the Dunning Golf Club business plan. [9]

I can ...

- ☐ Explain the main purposes of a business plan
- ☐ Evaluate a business plan.

1.3 Business ownership

Features of different types of business ownership

REVISED

When a business becomes incorporated, it has a separate and distinct legal entity that is independent of the business owners. **Sole traders** and **partnerships** are not incorporated, while **private limited companies** and **public limited companies** are incorporated, which means they have limited liability (see next section).

The main features of the different types of business ownership are shown in Table 1.2, together with their advantages (✓) and disadvantages (✗).

Partnership: A business owned by between 2 and 20 partners.

Sole trader: A business owned by one person.

Table 1.2 Types of business ownership

Feature	Sole trader	Partnership	Private limited company	Public limited company
Easy to set up	✓ Few forms to complete.	✓ Only needs a **deed of partnership** (a written agreement between partners).	✗ The Registrar of Companies requires legal documents, which take time to produce.	✗ The Registrar of Companies requires legal documents, which take time to produce.
Easy for the owner(s) to control	✓ The owner makes all the decisions.	✓ The partners (usually) make decisions between themselves. ✗ It is possible that the partners may disagree which would lead to problems making decisions. ✗ The profits will have to be shared between all the owners.	✓ Shareholders can restrict who can buy shares.	✗ Anybody can buy **shares**.
Continuity	✗ The business stops when the owner dies.	✗ A new deed of partnership will be needed when an owner leaves or joins.	✓ The business continues even if shareholders sell their shares or die.	✓ The business continues even if shareholders sell their shares or die.
Business information can be kept private	✓ No information about profits must be published.	✓ No information about profits must be published.	✗ The public can see information about the business.	✗ The public can see information about the business.
Raising finance	✗ This is limited because there is only one person to invest savings and banks may think they are risky to lend to. The business cannot sell shares to raise finance.	✗ Usually there are only a few partners to invest in the partnership and banks may think they are risky to lend to. Ability to raise finance may be limited as a result. ✗ The partnership cannot sell shares to raise finance.	✓ New shareholders can invest and banks are willing to lend. Larger amounts can be raised than sole traders and partnerships (usually).	✓ New shareholders can invest and banks are willing to lend. Large amounts of money can often be raised.

Feature	Sole trader	Partnership	Private limited company	Public limited company
Level of liability (risk)	✗ Owner has unlimited liability.	✗ The owners (partners) have unlimited liability.	✓ The owners (shareholders) have and benefit from limited liability.	✓ The owners (shareholders) have and benefit from limited liability.
Workload	✓ The owner makes all the decisions but may have to work long hours.	✗ The work is shared between the owners, but the fewer the partners, the greater the workload of each.	✗ Managers are employed to make decisions.	✗ Managers are employed to make decisions.

Now test yourself

TESTED

1 Which of the following is a feature of a public limited company? [1]
   (a) The business does not need to publish its business information.
   (b) The owners have limited liability.
   (c) The owners draw up a deed of partnership when the business is created.
   (d) The business cannot sell shares to raise extra finance.

2 Aaron Albright started a sole trader business manufacturing and fitting sun blinds. He began by selling the sun blinds to home owners. However, the business has grown and he now sells to business customers as well as fitting blinds in shops and offices. Aaron needs to produce more blinds to meet demand. He wants to move production to a larger factory than he currently uses but will need a big investment to do this. Aaron is working long hours and is worried about coping with a bigger business. He is considering taking on a partner who will contribute some money to finance the investment.

   Evaluate the advantages and disadvantages to Aaron of taking on a partner. [9]

Deed of partnership: A document stating who owns the partnership, how much money each partner has invested and their role in the business.

Private limited company (Ltd): Usually a smaller business, it can sell shares to invited people only.

Public limited company (plc): It can sell shares to anyone who wants to buy.

Share: Part ownership of a business.

I can ...

- ☐ State who owns the different types of businesses.
- ☐ State the advantages of different types of businesses.
- ☐ State the disadvantages of different types of businesses.
- ☐ Evaluate the benefits of changing the type of business ownership.

Exam tip

Questions which ask you to state and explain the advantages and disadvantages or the suitability of different types of businesses are very common.

Concept of limited liability

REVISED

When we talk about business liability, we are referring to the responsibility of the business' owners for debts incurred by the business. The owners of an unincorporated business, such as sole traders and partners, have **unlimited liability** – in other words, they are responsible for *all* the debts of the business. Shareholders who own private limited or public limited companies benefit from **limited liability**. The table below summarises the differences between limited and unlimited liability.

Limited liability: The owners of a business can only lose the money they have invested in a business if it fails.

Unlimited liability: The owner of a business is responsible for repaying all the debts of a business.

Table 1.3 Comparison of limited and unlimited liability

Issue	Limited liability	Unlimited liability
Effect on owner	• The shareholders who own the company do not have to use their own savings or other private possessions to pay off the debts of the company if the business fails.	• The owners must pay back all the debts of the business they own. • If the business goes bankrupt, the owners must sell any **assets** the business has. • If this sale does not raise enough to pay off the debts, the owner(s) can be ordered to use their savings or sell private possessions to raise the money needed to pay off the debts.
Effect on business	• It helps businesses to start up and raise extra finance to expand because people are prepared to invest, knowing that they are not risking all their personal possessions.	• People may be discouraged from setting up a business because of the risk to their savings and other personal assets. • This can limit the creation and expansion of sole trader and partnership businesses.
Other impacts	• Forming a business as a limited company can be complicated because various legal documents need to be prepared and sent to the Registrar of Companies.	• It is easier to start up as a sole trader or partnership because legal documents do not have to be sent to the Registrar of Companies.

Now test yourself

TESTED ☐

1 Which statement about limited liability is false? [1]
(a) The owner of a business who has limited liability cannot be ordered to sell private possessions to pay off debts if the business fails.
(b) The owner of a sole trader business has limited liability.
(c) Limited liability encourages people to invest in a business because it reduces their risk.
(d) The shareholders in private limited companies benefit from limited liability.

2 Dan Wynne and Barbara Tennyson run a road haulage business. They have a fleet of refrigerated lorries which they use for delivering frozen foods for their customers. They began the business with one lorry which they paid for with their savings. Dan and Barbara expanded the business by buying a further seven lorries, which they paid for mainly with loans from the bank. They also have an overdraft on their bank account. Dan and Barbara started the business as a partnership but changed it to a private limited company when they expanded.

Analyse the benefit to Dan and Barbara of changing their business to a private limited company. [6]

Assets: Items owned by the business, such as stock, buildings and vehicles, as well as less obvious things such as a good reputation.

Exam tip

Liability is about risk. Whether liability is limited or unlimited is a key point to stress in answers to questions about different types of businesses.

I can ...

- ☐ Explain what limited liability means.
- ☐ Explain what unlimited liability means.
- ☐ Analyse why limited liability is important for businesses.
- ☐ Analyse why unlimited liability is important for businesses.

Suitability of different types of ownership in different business contexts

REVISED

The most appropriate type of ownership for a business will depend on the needs of that particular business. A **start-up** business and an **established business** will have very different **finance** requirements and their type of ownership – sole trader, partnership, private or public limited company – will reflect that. Figure 1.5 summarises the main points about the suitability of different types of businesses.

Established business: A business that has been trading for some time.

Finance: The money used to start up or to expand a business, usually from savings and loans. It is used for capital items such as investment in buildings and machinery.

Start-ups: New businesses that are just beginning.

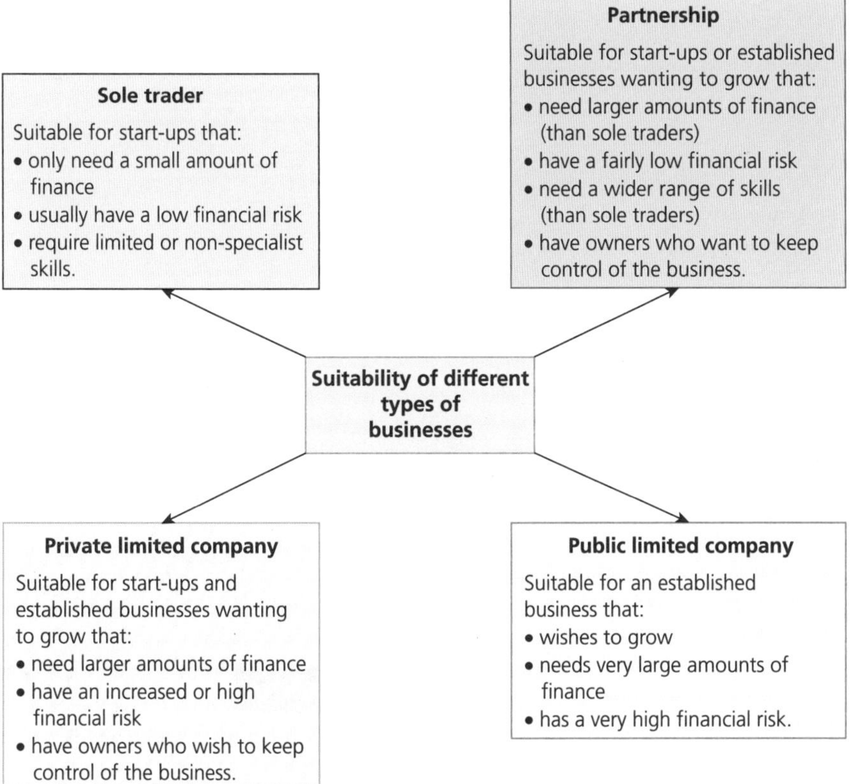

Figure 1.5 Types of businesses

Now test yourself

TESTED

In 1884, Michael Marks borrowed a small sum of money from a friend to start up a market stall business selling a range of cheap goods for a penny per item. By 1894, he wanted to open a permanent market stall selling a wider range of goods. Thomas Spencer, an experienced book-keeper with many business contacts and his own savings, became a partner in 1894. Marks & Spencer opened more and more shops and the business became a public limited company in 1926. Today Marks & Spencer has over 850 shops in more than 10 countries.

Evaluate how the different types of business ownership helped Marks & Spencer to develop. [9]

Exam tip

Think about the needs of the business owners with regard to finance, risk, skills and level of control of the business – and then decide which type of business ownership would most appropriately meet these needs.

I can ...

- ☐ State and explain the different needs of start-up and established businesses.
- ☐ Evaluate the type of business ownership required to meet the needs of a business.

1.4 Business aims and objectives

Aims and objectives of business

REVISED

Figure 1.6 summarises the different **business objectives**.

Business objectives: These are the aims of a business, and can include survival, profit, growth and providing a service.

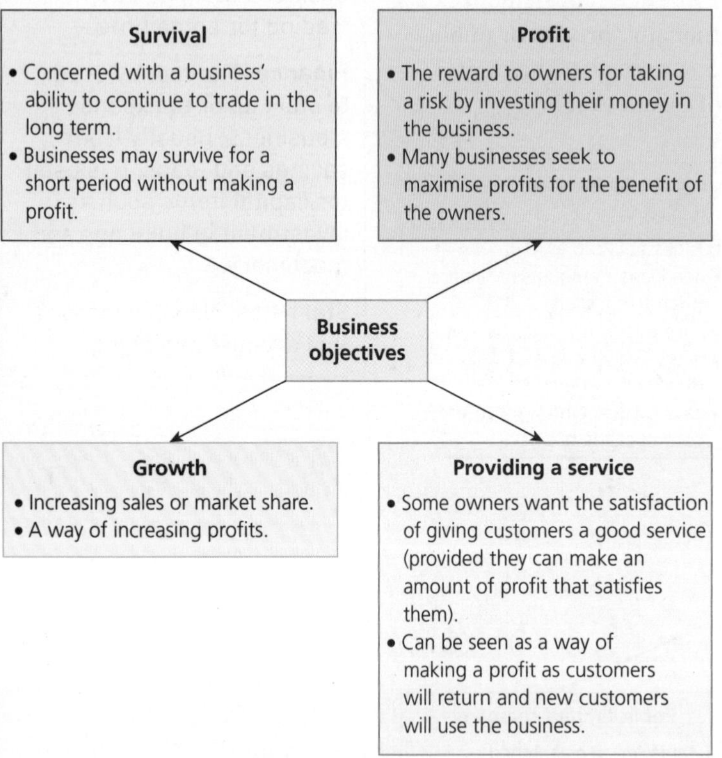

Figure 1.6 Business objectives

Now test yourself

TESTED

1 Which of these statements is **not** a business objective? [1]
   (a) A business seeks to maximise the profit it makes.
   (b) A business wishes to increase its sales.
   (c) A business cuts the wages of its workers.
   (d) A business wants to gain a good reputation by providing a good service.
2 In the table below, match the business objective with the description of the case study business.

Business objective	Description
1 Survival	a) E.ON, the energy company, has raised its prices even though costs have not risen.
2 Profit	b) Abdul has just opened a coffee shop in a small town where there are already four other coffee shops. He needs to establish the business in this competitive market by gaining sufficient customers to help it to stay in business in the longer term.
3 Growth	c) The Co-Operative supermarket chain aims to act responsibly and respectfully to its customers.
4 Providing a service	d) American business, Post Holdings, has bought the Weetabix brand from owners, China Bright Food.

Exam tip

Remember to apply your understanding of business objectives when you are asked to write about the objectives of a particular business in a case study.

I can ...

☐ State and explain and apply the main objectives of businesses.

How and why objectives might change as businesses evolve

REVISED

As businesses **evolve** they will have different objectives because:

- they are at different stages of their development
- their owners have different motivations
- they are influenced by different market conditions
- they are experiencing different economic conditions.

Figure 1.7 examines some of the reasons why businesses have different business objectives.

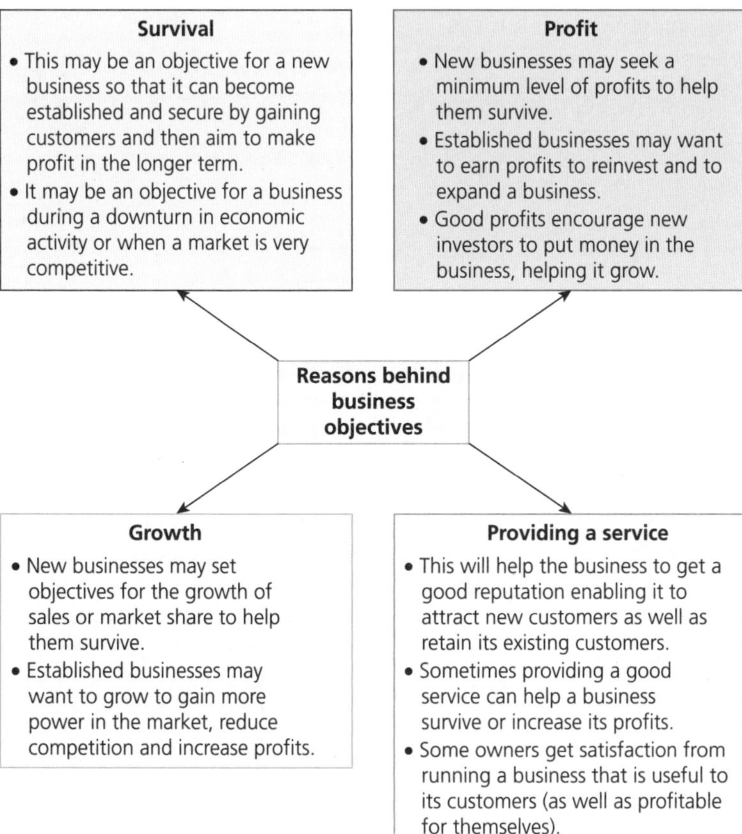

Figure 1.7 Reasons for different business objectives

Evolving: Refers to the way a business develops and changes over time, by becoming bigger or smaller and by selling different goods and services or a wider range, as well as selling in different places and in different ways.

Exam tip

Be ready to write about how the objectives of a business can alter as it changes or as economic conditions change. When writing your answer, remember to consider what motivates the owners of the business, too.

I can ...

- ☐ Explain different ways in which businesses evolve and how their objectives may change.
- ☐ Analyse why different business objectives are suitable for different businesses.

Now test yourself

TESTED

Ron Crosbie is a sole trader who sells and fits car tyres from a tyre centre in Ormskirk. Ron does make a profit but has never wanted to expand by opening other tyre centres. His business has a good reputation for competitive prices and a quality service and he believes this is what has kept him in business so long. The biggest threat came when Kwik Fit opened a tyre outlet in the town. Kwik Fit now owns over 570 outlets across the UK as well as mainland Europe after the company bought Speedy Tyres in France and Pit Stop in Germany. Kwik Fit expanded further by starting to sell insurance services.

Analyse the different objectives of Ron Crosbie Tyres and Kwik Fit. [9]

1.5 Stakeholders in business

Roles and objectives of internal and external stakeholder groups

REVISED

Table 1.4 lists the **internal** and **external stakeholders** of a business and states the role and objectives of each type of **stakeholder**. 'Role' refers to what a stakeholder may do in connection with the business, while 'objectives' refers to what the stakeholder wishes to achieve.

External stakeholders: The local community, suppliers, customers and government.

Internal stakeholders: The business owners and the people who work in the business.

Stakeholders: Groups or individuals who have an interest in a business.

Table 1.4 Roles and objectives of internal and external stakeholders

	Role	Objectives
Internal stakeholders		
Owners	• Provide finance to start up and expand the business. • They may manage or run the business or they may employ managers to run it on their behalf.	• Make profits.
Employees	• Produce goods and services.	• Satisfaction of having a job and earning an income. • Be treated fairly by employers. • Enjoyment of social aspects of working with colleagues.
External stakeholders		
Customers	• Buy goods and services.	• Enjoy the benefits provided by goods and services. • Pay affordable prices.
Suppliers	• Sell goods for resale or components and materials needed to manufacture goods or provide a service.	• Make sales. • Earn profits.
Government	• Help businesses, workers and communities.	• Encourage businesses as this leads to high employment and prosperous communities. • Government wants to encourage businesses because this increases the taxes paid to government.
Local community	• Provide workers. • Monitor and influence business activities.	• Have a local area which is prosperous, healthy and safe.

Now test yourself

TESTED

1 Which of these stakeholders of Debenhams plc will want to earn a wage from the business? [1]
(a) Customers of Debenhams plc.
(b) The government.
(c) Workers at Debenhams plc.
(d) The shareholders of Debenhams plc.

2 Cuadrilla is a fracking company which extracts gas from below ground. It has permission to drill at Roseacre Wood, a rural area in Lancashire north of the city of Preston and surrounded by several small villages. It has drill wells at the site. Cuadrilla needs to pump a lot of water in to the site, build roads and dig trenches for pipes. Some of the local community were involved in a campaign to stop planning permission being given for the wells, but others in the wider community area hope there will be increased employment opportunities as a result of Cuadrilla's plans.

State **two** internal and **two** external stakeholders in Cuadrilla plc. For each stakeholder, state their role and their likely objective. [8]

I can ...

- ☐ Define the term 'stakeholder.'
- ☐ State the main internal and external stakeholders of a business.
- ☐ State the role of each of the internal and external stakeholders.
- ☐ State the objectives of each of the internal and external stakeholders.

Exam tip

Always read questions carefully and obey the command in the question. The command word here is state. State simply means name – the stakeholders in this case. Stating the stakeholder's role means saying what they do, while stating their objective means saying what they want to achieve. In this type of question there is no need to add any discussion, for example, of whether the fracking will be good or bad for stakeholders.

Effect of business activity on stakeholders

REVISED

A business can affect stakeholders both positively and negatively. Table 1.5 gives examples of the **benefits of business activity** and **problems caused by business activity** for stakeholders that arise from the activities of a business.

Benefits of business activity: For stakeholders, these include profits, jobs and incomes, goods and services, sales, taxes and prosperity.

Problems caused by business activity: For stakeholders, these include financial losses, redundancy, poor goods and services, late or missed payments, bad publicity and negative impacts on the local environment and community.

Table 1.5 Benefits and problems for stakeholders arising from business activities

Stakeholder	Benefits of business activities	Problems from business activities
Owners	• Earn profits if the business is successful.	• May lose money invested in the business if it fails.
Employees	• Employed in a job role within the business and able to earn an income from the business.	• May be made redundant if the business does not do well or if their job is replaced by automation such as a robot. • Employment conditions may be unfair, leading to stress.
Customers	• Obtain products and services at good prices that satisfy their wants.	• May be sold poor quality goods and services. • May be over-charged for goods or services. • May experience poor customer service.
Suppliers	• Sell their goods to another business and earn profits from doing this.	• May lose money if the business does not pay for goods supplied. • Cash flow problems in the business may mean that they delay payment to their suppliers.
Government	• Receive tax revenue from the owners, workers, suppliers and customers of the business.	• Very large companies can become 'too big to fail' – the government may be criticised if the business fails and the government does not step in to help it to survive.
Local community	• People in the community can earn money from jobs with the business or because workers in the area have money to spend in their businesses.	• The community can be affected by negative externalities such as pollution and road congestion caused by the business.

Now test yourself

TESTED

Read again the Cuadrilla case study on page 19, then answer the following question.

Identify **one** internal and **one** external stakeholder in Cuadrilla (you may wish to choose the same stakeholders you wrote about in your answer to the data response question in the previous section). For each stakeholder, analyse **one** benefit and **one** problem which they may experience from the business activities of Cuadrilla plc. [8]

Exam tip

Learn at least one benefit and one problem experienced by each type of business stakeholder so that you are able to answer a question which focuses on any one of the stakeholders.

I can ...

☐ Analyse how each stakeholder in a business may be affected by it.

Effect of stakeholders on business

REVISED

Stakeholders can influence **business success**. Table 1.6 summarises ways in which each stakeholder can help a business to succeed or cause **business failure**.

Business failure: This can be indicated by losses, low sales, poor quality goods and services and a negative impact on the local community.

Business success: This may be measured in terms of profits, growth, sales, returning customers and a positive contribution to the local community.

Table 1.6 Stakeholder influences on business

Stakeholder	How the stakeholder may influence the success of a business	How the stakeholder may contribute to the failure of a business
Owners	● Investing enough money. ● Using the investment in ways that will help the business to grow and succeed.	● Not investing enough to make the business efficient. ● Failing to change the business when the market for its goods and services changes.
Employees	● Working hard to produce good quality goods or services at competitive costs.	● Producing poor quality goods or services. ● Demanding high wages as this will lead to higher costs. ● Disrupting production by industrial action.
Customers	● Purchasing goods and services. ● Creating a good reputation for the business by recommending it to others.	● Deciding to buy from competitors. ● Publicising instances of poor quality goods or bad service, leading to a poor reputation for the business.
Suppliers	● Providing supplies promptly and at competitive prices to help the business produce its goods and services cheaply and reliably.	● Supplying poor goods or services which lead to quality problems. ● Not supplying components or materials on time which can cause production delays.
Government	● Giving the business a grant to enable it to pay for investment or by giving it planning permission to develop or expand its facilities. ● Government may also be a customer of the business, buying goods and services from it.	● Reducing the business' profits by increasing taxes or by raising the National Minimum Wage so that wage costs increase. ● Preventing the expansion of the business by refusing planning permission.
Local community	● Providing the business with customers and supporting its plans for development.	● Opposing the business' plans for expansion or preventing production by not supporting its application for planning permission. ● This may lead to increased legal costs for the business as it fights for planning permission.

Now test yourself

TESTED ☐

Re-read the Cuadrilla case study (page 19), as well as the information below.

Cuadrilla will submit a planning application to allow it to develop the drilling site at Roseacre Woods. It intends to use very experienced employees to prepare its planning application. It knows that the local community are very much against planning permission for the site to be developed and that there are well-off, qualified and articulate people living in the area.

Evaluate the possible effects on **one** of the following stakeholders on the success of Cuadrilla's planning application:

- Employees of Cuadrilla [7]

or

- Local community. [7]

Exam tip

Evaluation is the most difficult skill to develop. You need to consider arguments that are both 'for' and 'against' and decide what will affect the importance of each. In the Cuadrilla case study, think about how well each of the two stakeholders involved will present their arguments and what skills and qualities they will need to present their case well.

I can ...

☐ Analyse and evaluate the effect that each stakeholder in a business can have on the business.

1.6 Business growth

Organic growth

REVISED

Figure 1.8 shows four ways in which **organic growth** can take place. Although the diagram shows four separate boxes, the examples of growth described in the boxes are interconnected. For example, a business may increase its **capacity** because it has increased its sales or a firm may increase its sales because its market share has increased as a result of a new advertising campaign.

Capacity: For a factory or shop, capacity refers to how much output it can produce or sell.

Organic growth: Concerned with the internal growth of a business, for example, by increasing its sales.

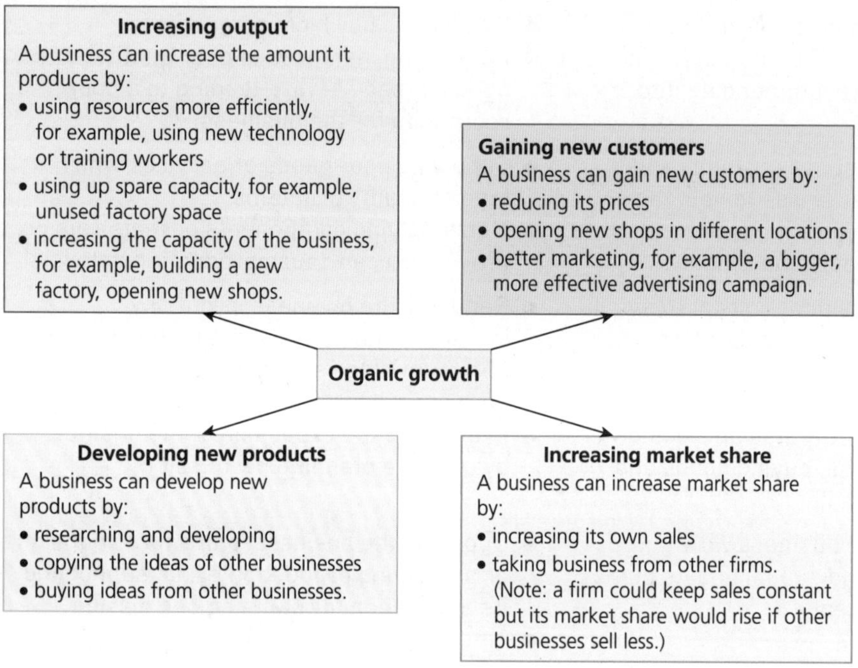

Increasing output
A business can increase the amount it produces by:
- using resources more efficiently, for example, using new technology or training workers
- using up spare capacity, for example, unused factory space
- increasing the capacity of the business, for example, building a new factory, opening new shops.

Gaining new customers
A business can gain new customers by:
- reducing its prices
- opening new shops in different locations
- better marketing, for example, a bigger, more effective advertising campaign.

Organic growth

Developing new products
A business can develop new products by:
- researching and developing
- copying the ideas of other businesses
- buying ideas from other businesses.

Increasing market share
A business can increase market share by:
- increasing its own sales
- taking business from other firms. (Note: a firm could keep sales constant but its market share would rise if other businesses sell less.)

Figure 1.8 Ways in which organic growth can occur in a business

Now test yourself

TESTED

Apple was started in 1976 and is now the largest company in the world. It began by making and selling desktop computers and its first order was for 50 computers sold at $666 each, bringing in revenue of $33,300. In 2016, its revenue had grown to $49.6bn – a huge increase, even allowing for price rises since 1976. During its history, Apple has taken over only a very small number of other businesses. Apple has researched and developed a range of successful products, including laptop computers such as the Macbook Pro, mobile phones (iPhone), tablet computers (iPad) and services such as Apple Pay. Apple has run some very effective marketing campaigns. It often introduces new products around September and advertises them heavily in the lead up to Christmas. Its advertising is often very innovative, using catchy music, a confident narrator and minimalist backgrounds in order to focus attention on its products.

1 What evidence is given in this case study for the growth of Apple? [1]
2 Analyse the reasons for the growth of Apple. [3]

Exam tip

Case studies are designed to provide clues and evidence to help you to answer the questions. Read them carefully so that you use the information in them to gain as many marks as possible.

I can ...

- ☐ Explain the meaning of organic growth.
- ☐ Analyse how the organic growth of a business can take place.

Now test yourself answers at www.hoddereducation.co.uk/myrevisionnotesdownloads

External growth

REVISED

Figure 1.9 illustrates the different kinds of **external growth** that can occur within a business. This example focuses on a furniture manufacturer. The boxes around the outside of the diagram show how the furniture manufacturer business is involved in a **merger** or **takeover** with other businesses, with the type of growth that occurs labelled next to the arrow. The benefits of each type of growth are shown inside each box. vv

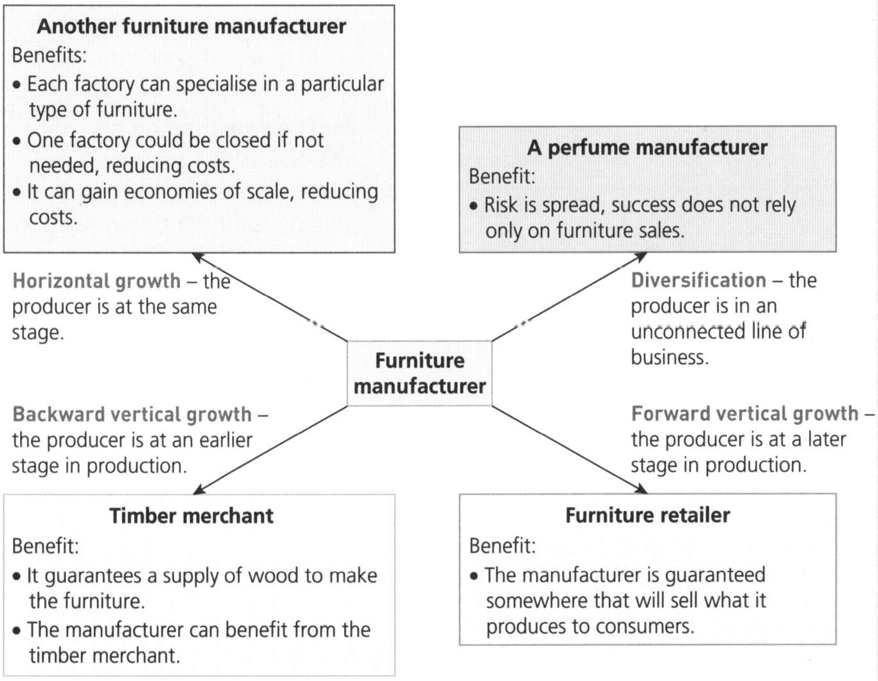

Another furniture manufacturer
Benefits:
- Each factory can specialise in a particular type of furniture.
- One factory could be closed if not needed, reducing costs.
- It can gain economies of scale, reducing costs.

Horizontal growth – the producer is at the same stage.

A perfume manufacturer
Benefit:
- Risk is spread, success does not rely only on furniture sales.

Diversification – the producer is in an unconnected line of business.

Furniture manufacturer

Backward vertical growth – the producer is at an earlier stage in production.

Timber merchant
Benefit:
- It guarantees a supply of wood to make the furniture.
- The manufacturer can benefit from the timber merchant.

Forward vertical growth – the producer is at a later stage in production.

Furniture retailer
Benefit:
- The manufacturer is guaranteed somewhere that will sell what it produces to consumers.

Figure 1.9 Types of external growth

Backward vertical growth: When a business merges with, or takes over, a business that supplies it with goods or services.

Diversification: When a business merges with or takes over another business with which it has no connection.

External growth: The growth of a business by takeover or merger.

Forward vertical growth: When a business merges with, or takes over, a business that it supplies goods or services to.

Horizontal growth: A merger or takeover where the two businesses are involved in a similar operation.

Merger: Where two or more businesses agree to join to become one business.

Takeover: Where a business takes a controlling interest in another business, for example, by buying more than 50% of the shares in it.

Now test yourself

TESTED

1 Which of the following statements describes a takeover? [1]
   (a) Orange and T-Mobile joined together to become EE.
   (b) Disney the film-maker bought the cartoon animation company, Pixar.
   (c) Honda Motor Company builds a factory to manufacture gear boxes for its cars.
   (d) Netflix increases its share of the market.

2 Identify the type of growth which takes place in each of the following and give a reason for your choice. [6]
   (a) A brewery takes over chain of public houses.
   (b) A bus company takes over a chain of fitness centres.
   (c) A food retailer merges with another food retailer.

Exam tip

Be ready to answer questions which ask you to identify the type of external growth described. Make sure you can explain the different reasons why businesses merge or takeover other businesses.

I can ...

- ☐ Explain the difference between a merger and a takeover.
- ☐ Identify the different types of external growth.
- ☐ Analyse the reasons for or benefits of different types of external growth.

2 Marketing

2.1 Role of marketing

Purpose of marketing within business

REVISED

Figure 2.1 shows the three main purposes of **marketing**.

When a business decides to market a product, it will need to consider these factors:

- Finance – how much finance is available to spend on research and development of the new product or an advertising campaign?
- Who the marketing is aimed at – young people may be more likely to respond to advertisements on social media. Different groups of people may require different products, for example, some older people may like a mobile phone that has large buttons and is easy to use; only rich people may be willing to pay high prices for top quality goods.
- Location of potential customers – which country or region of a country do they live and what language do they speak.

Marketing: Finding out the needs of consumers and demonstrating how a business fulfils those needs so that its sales increase.

Identifying and understanding customers
- Who are they (male or female, young or old, rich or poor), what do they want, where do they live?
- Answers to these questions can be found through market research.

Informing customers
- Advertise on TV, in papers, billboards, social media (Twitter, Facebook).
- How much advertising a business does will be influenced by what it can afford and who it needs to inform.

Main purposes of marketing

Increasing sales
- Sales can be increased by reducing price, introducing new products, selling in different places or by different methods (e.g. online or shops) and promotion, including advertising.
- Think of the 4Ps: price, product, place and promotion.

Figure 2.1 Main purposes of marketing

Exam tip

When answering a question on evaluation, make sure you use any evidence given in the case study to make a judgement. You might include further evidence in your answer if you have some or explain what further evidence would be useful.

Now test yourself

TESTED

Samsung wants to increase the sales of its mobile phones.

1 Explain **three** ways in which Samsung could increase its sales of mobile phones. [6]

2 Analyse **one** factor which will influence how Samsung markets its mobile phones. [3]

I can ...

- ☐ Explain what marketing is.
- ☐ Explain the purposes of marketing.
- ☐ Analyse the factors which influence how a business chooses to market its product.

2.2 Market research

Purpose of market research

REVISED

Market research is about identifying and understanding customer needs in order to produce goods and services to meet those needs. Figure 2.2 summarises what market research is about.

Market research is used to inform key business decisions, and so can influence whether a business succeeds or fails.

If a business does no market research, or conducts its research poorly, the chance of the business succeeding will be reduced. Any information gathered through market research must be interpreted correctly to:

- understand its significance to the business
- help marketing decision makers in the business choose the marketing strategy which best meets the needs of their **target market**.

Though market research costs money, this will, if the research is used effectively, be repaid to the business as sales revenue.

Market research: The collection of data on customer habits to help decision-making in marketing.

Target market: A group of customers to whom a business aims to sell its products. The target market may be other businesses as well as consumers.

Marketing involves the 4Ps:
Price, product, place and promotion (sometimes a fifth P, packaging, is added to the list) because the information it produces will help business to decide its marketing strategy. (See Section 2.4 for more detail on the 4Ps.)

↓

Market research aims to find out information about the target market:

- *Their age* – children or adults, young or old.
- *Their economic status* – rich or poor, do they want high or low quality goods or services.
- *Their culture* – what motivates them, what do they enjoy.
- *Where they are* –urban or rural areas, in the north, the Midlands or the south, in the UK or abroad.
- *What they want* in a product or service – style or function, large or small size, hot or cold.

↓

Good market research helps a business to be successful and avoid expensive mistakes by finding out:

- The *product* or service customers want.
- The *price* its customers are willing to pay.
- The *design* of the product that will be attractive to customers.
- *How many* products customers will buy and so how many it should buy-in or make.
- *How to target* customers – which media to use, what message to put out, what language to use.
- *Where and how* to sell its goods and services – through retailers, either online or on the high street, through personal sales representatives.

Figure 2.2 Market research

Exam tips

Evaluation questions ask you to make a judgement – whether something is good or bad, useful or not. You will need to weigh up these points and then come to a judgement. Remember to give a reason or reasons for your decision. Evaluation also requires analysis. For example, you may need to explain *why* information is useful to a business.

Now test yourself

TESTED

Next plc is considering introducing a new clothing range. The clothes will be targeted at women in the age group 16–25. Next plc has asked a market research company to research this market.

Evaluate the importance to Next plc of conducting market research before introducing a new range of clothing. [9]

I can ...

- ☐ Explain the term 'market research'.
- ☐ Explain the term 'target market'.
- ☐ Analyse the information that market research can produce for a business.
- ☐ Evaluate the usefulness of market research for a business.

Primary research methods

REVISED

Primary research is about collecting new data directly from people within the target market. Figure 2.3 summarises the main methods used to collect primary data and their advantages and disadvantages. Each method is a kind of survey. It will not be possible to reach everyone in the target market so usually a sample of representative people is chosen to get information from.

Primary research: Data that is collected first hand, often in the form of questionnaires, interviews and focus groups. Sometimes referred to as 'field' research.

Primary research methods

Questionnaire

A set of questions sent out to selected people in the post or asked online.

Advantages:

- Cheap to carry out.
- Easy to target customers, for example, people who buy cameras online.

Disadvantages:

- People may not understand the questions.
- People may not be interested in the product, so may answer dishonestly or not at all.

Interview

A person asks an individual or a group of people questions (in person or on the phone) and records their answers.

Advantages:

- The questions can be explained.
- It is easy to target certain types of consumers.

Disadvantages:

- It is an expensive method.
- Not everybody likes being interviewed.

Trialling

A product is sold for a short period, usually in one region of a country. If it sells well the business will go into full production.

Advantages:

- A good way to see if the product is what people want.
- Reduces the risk involved in producing large quantities.

Disadvantage:

- The people or area tested must be representative of the total market, otherwise the findings will not help the business.

Focus group

A small group of people are asked to use a product or think about an advertisement and to give their opinion. The feedback helps the business to re-design the product or advert.

Advantage:

- The people chosen will be representative of potential customers.

Disadvantages:

- It will only be a small group.
- It is usually costly to carry out.

Figure 2.3 Primary research methods

Now test yourself

TESTED

The Royal Society for the Protection of Birds (RSPB) runs several bird reserves around the country, where birds can nest and feed safely. Members of the RSPB provide money to pay for the reserves through annual subscriptions. In return they receive services such as free access to the reserves, shops, conferences and education services for schools. The RSPB plans to use an online questionnaire to get the views of members about the quality of its services. The questionnaire will pop up when members enter the RSPB website.

1 This online research is an example of: [1]
   (a) primary research
   (b) secondary research
   (c) a trial
   (d) interview data
2 Analyse **one** advantage to the RSPB of its plan to ask members to complete an online questionnaire. [3]

Exam tip

When you revise, try to learn 'trigger' words which will remind you of key terms and their advantages and disadvantages. For example: interviews = individual questions, explained, targeted, BUT expensive, disliked.

I can ...

- ☐ Explain what primary research is.
- ☐ State and explain the main methods of primary research.
- ☐ Analyse the usefulness to a business of different types of primary research.

Now test yourself answers at www.hoddereducation.co.uk/myrevisionnotesdownloads

Secondary research methods

REVISED

Secondary research involves using information that has already been created.

Table 2.1 summarises the main sources of secondary data and their advantages and disadvantages.

Secondary research: The collection of data using research and information provided by others, such as magazines, journals and the internet. Often called desk research.

Table 2.1 Secondary research methods

Method of secondary research	Description	Advantages	Disadvantages
UK Census data	• The national census finds out information about all UK households every 10 years. • It includes information about the numbers of people living in the household, their income and where they live.	• Information comes from a lot of people – almost the whole population of the country. • It is already collected and analysed, reducing the cost to business.	• Information has not been collected to meet the specific needs of the business. • The information will need careful interpretation.
Data from newspapers and magazines	• Articles in publications often describe people's interests and current fashions.	• Such information is up to date, cheap (involves only the cost of the newspaper or journal or may even be available free on the internet) and is a good source of ideas.	• Information will be general and not specific to the business.
Data from websites	• Information about other companies can be found, including what they sell and the prices they charge.	• Cheap to collect and readily available. Such data can help a business decide what to produce (and what not to produce) as well as the price to charge.	• The information will need careful interpretation by the business.
Internal data	• This is data collected by the business about, for example, its past sales and profits as well as customer feedback.	Cheap to collect, readily available and is specific to the business.	• Data is historical – it looks at what *has* happened, not what *will* happen.

Now test yourself

TESTED

Age UK is a charity which provides advice for older people. It needs to decide whether to open an Age UK office in Leamington Spa.

1 Explain the term 'secondary market research'. [1]
2 Analyse how information from the UK Census may help Age UK decide whether to open an office in Leamington Spa. [3]

I can ...

☐ Explain secondary market research.
☐ State and explain the different types of secondary research.
☐ State and explain the advantages and disadvantages of the different types of secondary research.

Exam tip

Exam questions may ask you to define terms or analyse advantages or disadvantages of different kinds of secondary research. You will usually need to apply your learning to a case study.

Appropriateness of different methods and sources of market research for different business purposes

REVISED

When choosing to conduct market research, a business must decide whether to use primary or secondary research or both. The decision will be influenced by the following factors:

- How much the business can afford to spend – some organisations will only be able to afford secondary research, while others may be willing to spend large amounts of money on primary research.
- What information is required – first-hand information from potential customers gained from, for example, an interview or a trial may be a good way to get opinions about a new product. Secondary information about people in the local community may be gained from the Census or from local newspapers. Information about competitors may be obtained from their websites.
- Location of customers – a questionnaire or telephone interview may be a good way of getting information from customers in another country. A local newspaper may provide information about the market in a particular town.
- How quickly the information is needed – it will be quicker to use secondary information than to have to prepare and carry out primary research.

Now test yourself

TESTED

Bolton Wanderers Football Club plan to introduce a new football strip which the team will wear and replicas will be sold through the club shop. The club is planning to get some ideas from fans before designing a strip and then showing it to fans to see if they like it or not.

1 Evaluate **two** methods of primary research which Bolton Wanderers Football Club should use to research the design for its new replica football strip. [9]

Jenny Jones has just finished a university degree in fashion design. She lives in Norwich and is considering starting up a small trader business making and selling dresses in shop premises in the city. She is planning to do some market research using information from the Census or from the websites of other businesses.

2 Evaluate the usefulness to Jenny of researching information from the websites of other dress-making businesses in Norwich. [9]

I can ...

☐ Evaluate the usefulness of different methods of market research.

Exam tip

You must answer the question set. You should refer to the advantages and disadvantages specific to the question, for example, about primary information or information from websites. You can also bring in ideas about other kinds of information, both secondary and primary, that the business would find useful, but which would not be provided by a research method mentioned in the question. You may also need to stress the importance of research for the business.

Use and interpretation of qualitative and quantitative data in market research

REVISED

Qualitative data is usually collected using primary research as it involves finding out the opinions of customers who use the product or service. For example, a business may want to find out why people like or dislike the taste of the sweets its sells.

- An advantage of qualitative data is that it helps a business to understand what customers are thinking and what they want.
- A disadvantage of qualitative data is that information may only be provided by a limited number of people.

Quantitative data provides facts, for example, about what people do, what they spend or where they shop. A business may want to know how often a person goes to the cinema, for instance.

- An advantage of quantitative data is that it is easy to analyse. It can be gathered from a lot of people.
- A disadvantage of quantitative data is that it limits how much people can say about what they like or dislike.

Qualitative data: Data based on the opinions of those being asked.

Quantitative data: Data collected that is based on facts or numbers; it is usually easier to analyse than qualitative data.

Now test yourself

TESTED

A software company is planning to develop a new computer game aimed at teenagers. It is considering using research which will produce qualitative data.

Analyse **one** benefit to the software company of using research that will produce qualitative data. [3]

Exam tip

In an exam question you may be asked to focus on qualitative or quantitative data or both. Make sure your answer focuses on the *data* obtained and not on the different research methods.

I can ...

- ☐ Explain the difference between qualitative and quantitative data.
- ☐ Analyse the benefits of qualitative and quantitative data.

2.3 Market segmentation

Use of segmentation to target customers

REVISED

The market for a product or service can be divided into segments, known as **market segmentation**, as shown in Figure 2.4. People in different segments often want different kinds of products or services. Businesses need to know this so that they can target their products at the different needs of customers in each segment. When a business targets the different segments in its market, it will need to consider:

- whether to produce different products for different markets – the business may consider offering male/female versions or basic and more sophisticated models
- what price to charge – high or low
- how to promote the products – the type of media to use and what message this method may give
- where to locate shops – town centre, shopping mall, holiday resort – and whether to sell online or not.

Market segmentation: Splitting the market for a product or service into different parts or segments.

Exam tip

Learn as many examples of how businesses target customers in different market segments. This will help you to analyse and evaluate any case studies presented to you in the examination.

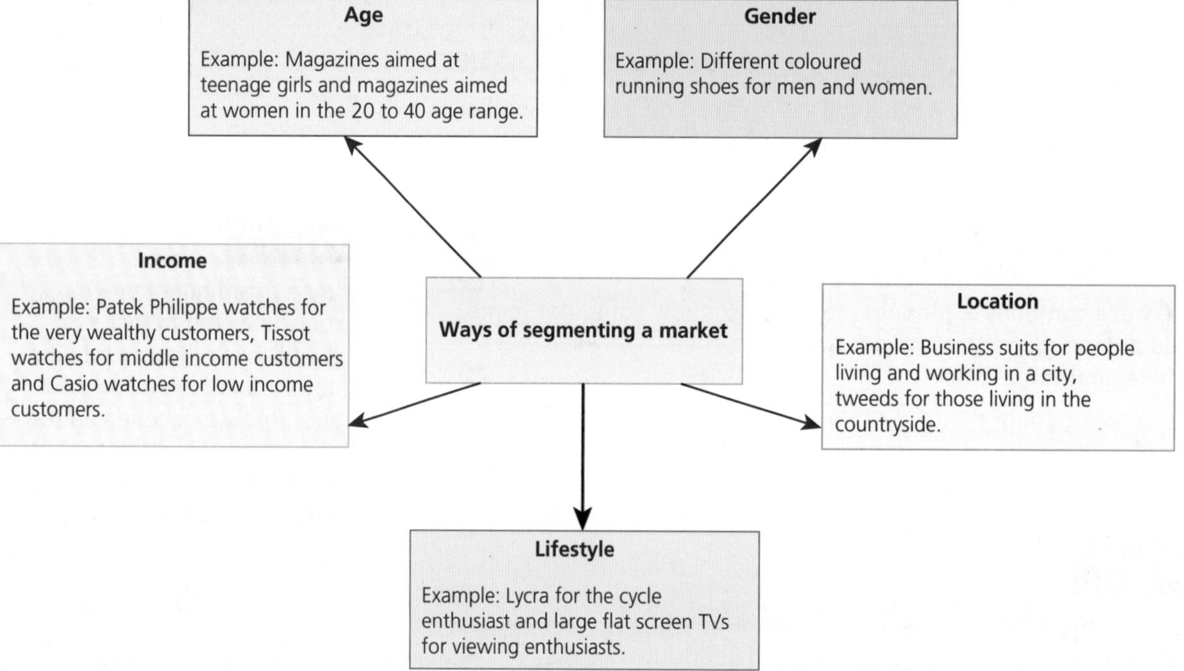

Figure 2.4 Segmenting a market

Now test yourself

TESTED

The Tesco loyalty card is called the Tesco Clubcard. When customers sign up for a Clubcard, they are asked to give Tesco information about, for example, their income, gender and age. Tesco use this information to target the different segments of their market. Wealthy customers may be sent offers about smoked salmon, while less well-off customers may be sent offers for more basic food stuffs such as baked beans.

1. Explain what is meant by the term 'market segmentation'. [2]
2. Analyse the benefit to Tesco of targeting customers, as described in the case study. [3]
3. Analyse **one** other way in which Tesco may target its customers. [3]

I can ...

- ☐ Explain, with examples, the meaning of the term 'market segmentation'.
- ☐ Explain how a business can target customers in different market segments.
- ☐ Analyse and evaluate the suitability of products for different market segments.

2.4 The marketing mix

The marketing mix refers to the 4 Ps of marketing – **p**roduct, **p**rice, **p**romotion and **p**lace – which are used together to market a product or service. Each 'P' is looked at in turn in this section, followed by a look at how they mix together.

Importance of the '4 Ps' of marketing – product and stages of the product life cycle

REVISED

Market research will inform businesses what customers want. The business must **design**, **invent** or **innovate** so that it is producing the product(s) or services that customers want to buy. These three processes are explained below:

Table 2.2 Processes involved in the development of a product or service

Activity	Meaning	Example
Design	When a business plans what a product will do (its function) and what it will look like (its style).	The Ford Focus is designed to meet the needs of C-segment consumers (lower middle class workers such as junior managers and skilled working class workers such as plumbers and electricians). These consumers have a median age of 42 and a household income of around £50,000. They want features such as automatic parallel parking, rain-sensing windshield wipers, parking cameras and keyless entry, among others.
Invention	When a business comes up with a new product or service.	Firms are working on mobile phones that can be charged without having to be plugged in.
Innovation	When a business improves a product which already exists.	The Samsung 8 mobile phone is an improvement on the Samsung 7.

The **product life cycle** refers to the four stages of life that a product usually goes through.

Figure 2.5 shows the product life cycle and explains each of the stages.

Advertising will be high during the **introduction** stage to ensure customers know about the product. During the **growth** phase, advertising is used to reinforce awareness of the product. In **maturity**, additional advertising may be used to keep sales high. In **decline**, buyers may be encouraged with special offers to buy stocks of goods the business has left over. The firm could also try to find new uses for the product to extend its sales and life cycle.

Decline: When sales are falling as the product or service is seen by customers to be old and they switch to new products or services.

Design: An important element in a number of different products, especially where style and technology work together.

Growth: When sales are growing strongly as the new product or service becomes known.

Innovation: The improvement of an original idea, which will often involve using new processes.

Introduction: When a product or service is first on sale.

Invention: The introduction of a totally new product or service.

Maturity: When sales are at their highest level.

Product life cycle: The life of a product, usually shown as a graph divided up into four stages: introduction, growth, maturity and decline.

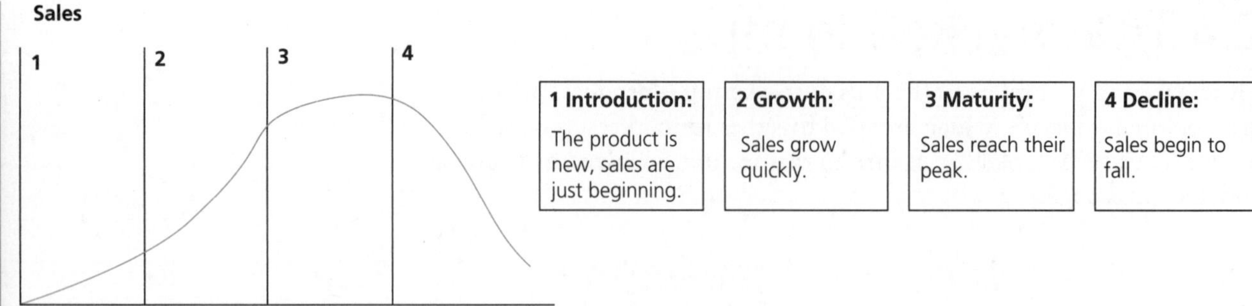

Figure 2.5 The product life cycle

Now test yourself

TESTED

Lego was first made and sold in 1949. The building blocks were based on Kiddicraft Self-Locking Building Bricks which had been created by Hilary Page. Duplo, which are larger building bricks, were introduced to suit younger children. During the 1990s, sales of Lego began to fall and some thought that decade would possibly see the end of Lego's product life cycle. However, Lego introduced new models based on characters from popular films and books such as Harry Potter and Winnie the Pooh. There is now a Lego board game and a film involving Lego characters. Lego's sales and profits are now very high.

1 Using the case study, identify **one** example of:
   (a) invention
   (b) innovation
   (c) design. [3]
2 Analyse how Lego has managed to extend the life cycle of its bricks beyond the period of decline in the 1990s. [3]

Exam tip

If you prefer to remember things in a visual form, learn diagrams such as the product life cycle diagram and use it in an examination to remind you of the different stages of the product life cycle.

I can ...

- ☐ Explain the main processes involved in developing products – design, invention and innovation.
- ☐ Explain the main stages of the product life cycle.
- ☐ Explain how a business may extend a product's life cycle.

Importance of the '4 Ps' of marketing – pricing methods

REVISED

Figure 2.6 summarises the five pricing methods that you need to know.

All pricing decisions are about making a profit. Businesses must consider the following when deciding what price to charge for a product:

- how new the product is
- the quality of the product
- the number and nature of the competitors
- how well customers know the product already
- what stage of the product life cycle the product is at
- the costs of producing the product.

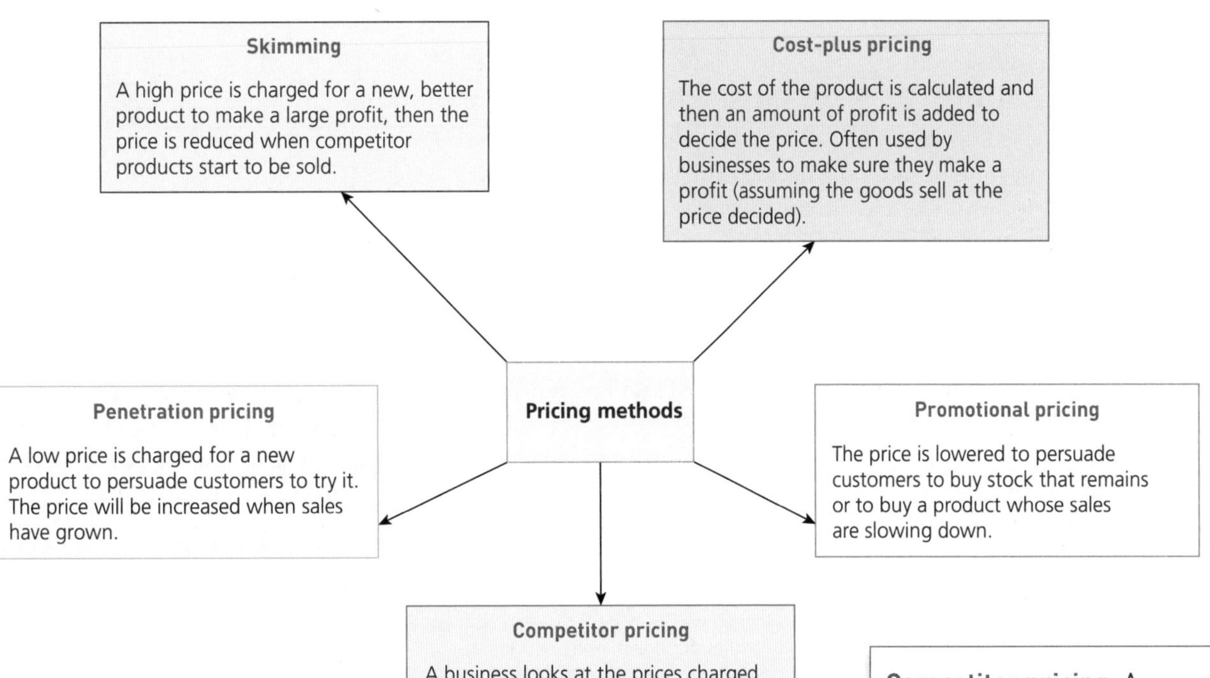

Figure 2.6 Pricing methods

Now test yourself

TESTED

Recommend **one** method of pricing which would be appropriate in each of the following situations. Give a reason for your recommendation.

1. Julie Roberts is opening a hairdressing salon in York. There are several other hairdressers in the part of the city where her shop is located. [3]
2. Vauxhall Motors has decided to introduce a new model of its popular car, the Astra. It wishes to sell off the old models of the Astra that it has already produced. [3]
3. Apple is introducing a new version of its iPad, which it claims has more features than previous versions and other tablet computers. [3]

Exam tip

When you are asked to make a recommendation, state your recommendation first and then give a reason or reasons for your decision. Usually more marks are given for the reason than the recommendation.

You would not normally be asked to make recommendations about more than one pricing decision in the exam. Here you have been asked for three in order to provide you with practice at recommending different methods of pricing.

Competitor pricing: A price is set based on prices charged by competitors for a similar product.

Cost-plus pricing: A pricing method that adds a percentage for profit to the total costs of making a product. This gives the selling price.

Penetration pricing: A price is set that is lower than those of competitors. Often used by new businesses to break into the market. It is a short-term strategy only.

Promotional pricing: Prices are reduced to give products a boost or to sell off old stock.

Skimming: Where a new product is more advanced than that of its competitors, a price is set high as consumers are willing to pay higher prices to own the newest technology. Also referred to as 'creaming'.

I can ...

- [ ] List the main pricing methods.
- [ ] Evaluate when each of the main pricing methods is useful.

Importance of the '4 Ps' of marketing – promotion: point of sale and advertising

REVISED

Promotion is about informing customers about what is for sale and persuading them to buy. The two main areas you need to know are:

- **Point of sale promotion** – a benefit the customer will receive when they buy the product.
- Advertising – giving the customer information about the product and persuading them to buy it.

Figure 2.7 summarises the main kinds of point of sale promotion and **promotional advertising media**:

POINT OF SALE PROMOTIONS

Price reductions (or 'sales')
To sell off old stock, for example, old models of cars, winter clothes as spring approaches. The disadvantage is that the business will make less profit (or even a loss) than if the product had been sold at a higher price.

Competitions
A person who buys a product is also entered in to a competition, for example, a voucher for a free holiday could be included in a number of bags of crisps. Customers 'win' by finding a voucher.

Loss leaders
Some goods are sold at a loss to encourage customers to come to the shop in the hope that they will do all their shopping there. For example, Tesco may sell petrol cheaply to attract customers and it will make its profits on the groceries those customers buy.

Free samples
These are given to tempt people to buy the product, for example, customers may be offered small pieces of cheese in a supermarket so they can try it.

ADVERTISING

Social media
A cheap way of communicating with large numbers of people as well targeting customers. Facebook and Twitter are good examples of this. However, not everyone uses social media.

Websites
A lot of information can be provided for potential customers, including written information, diagrams and videos. Content type depends on how much the business can afford to spend. It costs a business money to keep its website up to date.

Television
This is often expensive, but TV advertising is good for reaching a wide audience. Advertisers will know what channels and programmes potential customers watch.

Print media
This includes newspapers (local and national), magazines and leaflets. Businesses can target their market, for example, a local plumber would use a local newspaper, a supermarket chain a national paper, a fast food outlet could post leaflets through doors in the local area. However, many people do not read newspapers and leaflets are often ignored.

Radio
This is cheaper than TV and usually suitable for local advertising but products cannot be seen.

Figure 2.7 Point of sale promotion and promotional advertising

When a business wishes to promote a product, it will be influenced by the following:

- What the business can afford.
- The target audience – who and how many customers.
- The aim of the promotion – to sell off old stock, tempt new customers, etc.

Point of sale promotions: Sales offers available when purchasing a product. Promotions include price reductions, competitions, free samples and loss leaders. Loss leaders are goods offered at a low price. Although the business makes a loss on these products, it is hoped that while customers are buying these products, they will be tempted to buy other more profitable goods so that overall the shop makes the profit it needs.

Promotional advertising media: The ways in which a company can advertise its goods, such as social media, websites, print media, television and radio.

Now test yourself

TESTED

Recommend **one** type of media that could be used in each of these situations:

1 Regent Seven Seas Cruises offers luxury accommodation, top quality food and comprehensive services on its cruises. The cruises, which are very expensive, are aimed at wealthy people. Many buyers will be retired. [3]

2 Coca-Cola is running a campaign aimed at 16–25 year olds based on the theme of sharing and enjoying a good time together. [3]

3 Jacobs Biscuits has developed a new kind of cracker to eat with cheese. Recommend the point of sale method of promotion that it should use. [3]

Exam tip

Pick out key words to help you to remember different advertising mediums in the exam. For example, when considering television as an advertising medium, 'expensive' is a key disadvantage, while 'wide audience' and 'familiar with channels potential customers will watch' are good reminders of the advantages. Select your own key words for other point of sale promotions and advertising methods.

I can ...

- ☐ Explain the main methods of point of sales promotion.
- ☐ Explain the main media used for advertising, including an advantage and disadvantage of each.
- ☐ Evaluate when to use each method of point of sales promotion and each type of media.

Importance of the '4 Ps' of marketing – place: distribution of products and services

REVISED

Physical distribution is the movement of goods from the producer to the consumer. Figure 2.8 shows the different physical distribution channels in which goods can be moved from the producer to the consumer.

Physical distribution: The distribution of a good or service using a physical presence such as a shop or office.

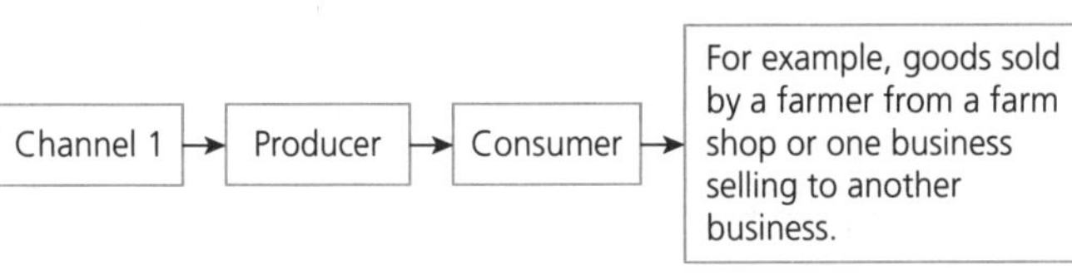

Channel 2 → Producer → Retailer → Consumer → For example, goods sold by an electronics company to a big retail chain such as Currys.

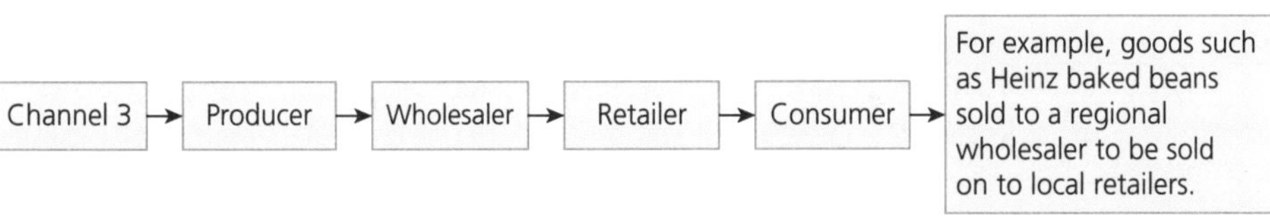

Figure 2.8 Physical distribution channels

The advantages of the three channels are as follows:

- Channel 1 – by missing out wholesalers and consumers, the producer makes more profit, rather than sharing it with a wholesaler and/or retailer.
- Channel 2 – selling directly to the retailer means the producer can benefit from keeping some of the profit that would have been made

by the wholesaler, while being confident the retailer will be able to market the goods to consumers.

- Channel 3 – a wholesaler can break up bulk stock and offer retailers the goods in the quantities that they can afford, and which they can sell, so more retailers are willing to sell the goods.

Digital distribution is when the product can be downloaded by the consumer directly from the seller, as in the case of books from Amazon onto a Kindle or music from Spotify onto a MP3 player.

Digital distribution: The distribution of goods and services digitally by downloading from a website.

Table 2.3 Advantages and disadvantages of digital distribution

Advantages of digital distribution	Disadvantages of digital distribution
The consumer can buy the product 24/7.	Physical goods cannot be distributed digitally.
It is a method of selling, without the costs of physical shops or transport.	It is a very competitive market as consumers can compare prices and products online.
	Customers who do not own a computer will be unable to buy online.
	Some customers do not like sharing their bank or credit card details online.

Now test yourself

TESTED

1 Dulux produces paints for indoor and external use. It sells:
- some paint directly to large retailers
- some paint to wholesalers who then sell it on to retailers.

(a) Analyse **one** advantage to Dulux of each of these methods of selling its paint. [2 x 3]

(b) Analyse **one** disadvantage to Dulux of selling its paint to wholesalers. [3]

2 LV Insurance sells many insurance policies online. Explain **one** advantage to LV Insurance of selling its policies online. [2]

Exam tip

Always state an advantage and then give a detailed explanation as to why it is an advantage. The same advice applies when writing about disadvantages.

I can ...

- ☐ Explain the difference between physical and digital distribution.
- ☐ State examples of physical and digital distribution.
- ☐ Explain the different channels of physical distribution.
- ☐ Explain the benefits of the different methods of physical distribution.
- ☐ Explain the advantages and disadvantages of digital distribution.

How the '4 Ps' of the marketing mix work together *and* Use of the marketing mix to inform and implement business decisions

REVISED

The 4 Ps of the **marketing mix** work together. When making decisions about the marketing mix, businesses must consider:

- the type of product they are selling
- the cost of the product
- the stage of the product life cycle of the product
- the target market
- the funds available for marketing.

Marketing mix: The mix of different parts of the marketing campaign – price, product, place and promotion (the 4 Ps).

Table 2.4 shows how the 4 Ps may mix together at different stages of the product life cycle of a mobile phone. All 4 Ps need to be used and be consistent with each other. Price skimming should be used only if the product is significantly better or different to those of competitors. It would not make sense to introduce a new product without also using promotional advertising to make customers aware of the product and advertising is necessary when a new product is introduced.

Table 2.4 The marketing mix and its effect on the product life cycle of a mobile phone

	Product life cycle stage			
Marketing mix	**Introduction**	**Growth**	**Maturity**	**Decline**
Product	• Introduce a new, high-tech phone.	• The phone does not change. • Begin the process of innovating and designing a model to replace the phone.	• Add new styles of the phone to attract a wider range of customers. • Continue the design and development process.	• Introduce new features to attract sales, for example, a larger memory or a better camera. • Be ready to introduce the new model once sales of the current phone can no longer be extended.
Price	• Use price skimming to make high profits from the phone, because some consumers will be willing to pay the high price.	• Reduce price to maintain sales.	• Maintain a stable price.	• Use promotional 'reduced' pricing to extend sales of the phone.
Place	• Sell through exclusive shops to stress the product's quality and to be able to sell at a high price.	• Sell through a wider range of shops and online to increase custom.	• Continue sales through a wide range of outlets.	• Continue sales through a wide range of outlets but reduce sales in outlets that are not selling many of the phones.
Promotion	• Use targeted advertising to generate interest in the product and stress its quality and exclusivity to people who are interested in new technology.	• Advertise widely to stress the benefits of the phone to a wider market.	• Continue to advertise to highlight differences of the phone to its competitors.	• Advertise to raise awareness of price reductions. • Give special offers such as free phone cases with the phone to encourage people to buy.

It is possible to judge the effectiveness of a marketing mix by asking the following questions:

- Have total sales increased and if so, by how much?
- Has the stock of products been sold off?
- Has the number of people who buy a good or service increased and if so, by how many?
- Has the business been able to increase the price or has it reduced the price?
- Has total sales revenue increased or decreased and by how much?
- Has the profit made by the business increased or decreased and by how much?

Now test yourself

TESTED

Large supermarket chains such as Morrisons, Tesco and Sainsbury have traditionally achieved success by selling mainly high quality brands at prices which were not necessarily cheap but which were competitive with each other. Their advertising campaigns stressed their quality and why they were better than their competitors. Following the recession of 2008 and 2009, many people lost their jobs and their income fell. The large supermarket chains were affected by the development of the 'no frills' supermarkets such as Aldi and Lidl, which offered a smaller range of goods, sometimes of lower quality than those at the large supermarkets, and at lower prices.

Analyse how the large supermarkets such as Morrisons, Tesco and Sainsbury may have changed their marketing mix to respond to this competition from the 'no frills' supermarkets. You should refer to product, price, promotion and place in your answer. [4 x 3]

I can ...

- ☐ Explain how the 4 Ps of the marketing mix work together.
- ☐ Analyse and evaluate the factors which influence decisions made by a business about the marketing mix it should use.
- ☐ Analyse and evaluate the effectiveness of marketing mix strategies.

Exam tip

Read the question carefully and answer the question set. If the question is only about one of the 4 Ps, your answer should only refer to that P. If it is about the marketing mix, refer to all 4 Ps in your answer.

Interpretation of market data

REVISED

Most businesses collect **market data** to help them to make decisions. Using and interpreting data means that decisions are *informed* – not just guesses about what is needed or what is happening. Data which can help marketing decisions is described in Table 2.5.

Market data: Information that can help marketing decisions. It includes data on such things as market share, changes in demand and the effect of promotions.

Market share: The percentage of total sales of a product that a business has made. For example, if a business sells 20,000 products and the total market for a product is 50,000 then the business has a market share of 40% (20,000 ÷ 50,000 x 100)

Target market: A group of consumers to whom the business tries to sell its products. It can be based on such areas as gender, age and lifestyle and will influence the methods of advertising and promotion that are used.

Table 2.5 Use of data to aid marketing decisions

Example of data	Information provided	Example use of data
Changes in demand	Data can shows if demand for a product is rising, falling or is unchanged.	Inform possible changes to: ● price – increase or reduce ● advertising – more or less needed ● the type of advertising ● promotional offers ● introduce a new product.
Target market	Who the customers are. What the customers want. Any changes in the target market, for example, increase in older people who are interested in the product.	To decide: ● the design of the product ● how much to charge for the product ● where, when and how to advertise ● which retail outlets to use ● which promotional offers, if any, to use.
Market share	The percentage of the total sales in a market of the business, and how this may be changing.	To help decide whether to change or to maintain the current marketing mix.
Product changes (introduced by a business or its competitors)	This will indicate if consumers want different products and if those of competitors are more or less successful.	The first decision will be whether or not the business needs to introduce a new product to match consumer needs and/or competitor products.
Effect of promotion	How the promotion is affecting sales and profits.	Use data to evaluate the effectiveness of any current promotion and make changes if necessary.

Now test yourself

TESTED ☐

Joe Allen runs a market stall in Nantwich, one of several market towns in the county of Cheshire. The market is open on Tuesdays, Thursdays and Saturdays. Nantwich is a prosperous town with lots of retired people living in the area, many of whom have incomes that are above the national average. In the past, running his stall on just three days a week brought in enough income for Joe to support his family and gave him time to work as a volunteer on environmental projects. Joe has targeted sales at young families whose incomes are around the national average. He buys vegetables from the local fruit and vegetable wholesale market. His prices are generally lower than those in the supermarkets. Sales figures for the past year show a 15 per cent decline and his profits have fallen by 20 per cent, while competition from supermarkets has increased.

Recommend how Joe might change his marketing mix in response to the fall in sales and profits. [9]

Exam tip

Any data provided in a case study is there to help you to answer questions, so try to make as much use of this information as possible.

I can ...

- ☐ Explain the main types of market data.
- ☐ Interpret market data and its impact on a business.
- ☐ Recommend marketing decisions based on market data.

3 People

3.1 Role of human resources

Identifying and meeting human resource needs

REVISED

Businesses need to identify what **human resources** and **functions** they need when they start up and throughout the lifetime of the business. **Identifying human resource needs** enables a business to create a **personnel plan**. This will include:

- how many workers it needs to employ
- the type of workers it needs – skilled or unskilled, managers, full time or part time, where they will work and at what time they will work
- how the business will get the best out of its workers.

Table 3.1 Factors influencing the human resource needs of a business

Factor	Influence on the human resource need
What it produces	Are skilled or unskilled workers needed, or a mix of both?
How much it produces	How many workers will the business need?
The method of production	Can machines rather than workers be used?
When production takes place	Are workers needed seven days a week or only on specific occasions?
The 'functions' or 'jobs' to be completed	What type of workers are needed – finance, production, marketing, human resources.
The budget available to the business	How much can be spent on workers?

Functions: The different types of work that need to be done in business, for example, in production, finance and marketing.

Human resources: The workers employed by a business.

Identifying human resource needs: The act of thinking about the purposes of human resources and how many and what types of workers will be needed.

Personnel plan: A plan detailing the employees a business needs – how many, whether they will be full or part time workers, the skills they should have and when they will work.

Now test yourself

TESTED

While in the Premier League, Bolton Wanderers football club earned a lot of money from gate money and the TV companies paid for the rights to televise games. The Club had paid big transfer fees and high wages to recruit new players and its 'backroom' staff such as coaches, specialist medical staff, player scouts and sales staff in its shops. Relegation led to severe financial trouble for the club as it now had big debts and a much-reduced income from attendance and TV. New owners bought the Club and had to reduce spending on human resources, affecting its chances of success.

Evaluate the impact of relegation and the reduction in income on the human resource needs of Bolton Wanderers Football Club. [9]

Exam tip

When revising, try learning information as a list, e.g. things that a business needs to consider when identifying its staffing needs. You could reduce the list to single words or short phrases, for example, what, how much, production method, when, functions, budget. In the exam, try to recall the list to help you write your answer.

I can ...

- ☐ Explain what is meant by human resources and the human resource needs of a business.
- ☐ State and explain the main influences on the human resource needs of a business.
- ☐ Evaluate how human resource needs may be affected by changes affecting the business.

3.2 Organisational structures and different ways of working

Different organisational structures

REVISED

Organisational structures can be classed as either 'tall' or 'flat'.

Organisation structure: How people and departments are arranged within a business.

Tall organisational structures have many layers of staff from top to bottom. Here there are eight layers, including the board of directors at the top, and down to shop-floor workers at the bottom.

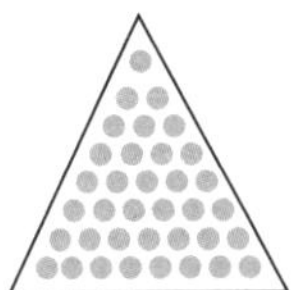

Figure 3.1 Tall organisational structure

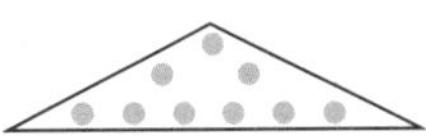

Figure 3.2 Flat organisational structure

Flat organisational structures will only have a few layers, maybe as little as two or three. There may be a board of directors at the top, one layer of managers and the shop floor workers.

Table 3.2 summarises the advantages of tall and flat organisation structures and what type of business situation they may be suitable for.

Table 3.2 Different types of organisation structure

	Tall structure	Flat structure
Advantages	• There are clear lines of communication from the people at the top to the people at the bottom of the organisation. • Managers tend to have only a few people that they are responsible for. • There will be opportunities for people to gain promotion within the organisation, which can be good for motivation.	• Managers tend to delegate responsibilities to the workers they have responsibility for, which is good for motivation. • Workers are likely to talk to a wider range of colleagues, so structure is good for generating ideas.
Disadvantages	• Subordinates may feel they are too controlled by their line manager which can stifle motivation and creativity. • Workers may only talk to immediate colleagues and may be less sympathetic or supportive to workers in other areas of the business.	• There are not always clear lines of communication and some workers may miss out on information which would help them and the business. • Managers may have a large number of workers to oversee. • Promotion opportunities may be few and may be unclear to workers, which may reduce motivation.
Suitability	• Tall structures suit large organisations, such as a large hospital. • Tall structures suit non-creative businesses where workers perform limited, clear tasks, for example, a building company.	• Flat structures are suitable for creative businesses, such as computer game design. • Flat structures are good for smaller businesses, because they can help workers feel valued.

Now test yourself

TESTED

Vauxhall Cars employs over 2000 workers at its site in Ellesmere Port, where it produces the Astra car. The organisation is divided into departments, the largest of which is the Operations Department, which is responsible for the assembly of the cars. Workers are divided into teams, each with a specific responsibility. One person may be responsible for doors, another for engines and so on. There are environmental teams who look after the cleanliness and safety of the plant and quality control teams.

Squarespace is a small US business which creates websites. It employs several webpage designers who create websites for their clients.

For each of the businesses above, recommend the type of organisational structure – tall or flat – which the business should use. Give reasons for your recommendations. [6]

I can ...

- ☐ Explain what is meant by an organisational structure.
- ☐ Explain the difference between tall and flat organisational structures.
- ☐ Explain the advantages and disadvantages of tall and flat organisational structures.
- ☐ Recommend when a tall or flat organisational structure is most appropriate for a business.

Exam tip

In the examination, expect questions that ask you to explain the difference between tall and flat structures, the advantages of each, and evaluation questions which ask you when it will be suitable to have a tall or flat structure.

Terminology of organisation charts

REVISED

The **organisation chart** below is for J.J. Jewellery, a sole trader business owned by Joe Johnson. Joe is responsible for the business, its finances and its accounts. The business makes its own jewellery and sells it through a shop, also owned by Joe Johnson, in the town of Bowton. The jewellery is designed by Amna Johnson, Joe's wife. It is made in a workshop by a team of three. Vafi Oman, Amna's brother, manages the production team. The shop is run by Myiesha Oman, Amna's sister. There are four shop assistants. Zac Doyle is a part-time buyer who buys jewellery from other manufacturers to sell in the shop.

Organisation chart: A diagram that shows how the workers are organised in a business and who is in charge of whom.

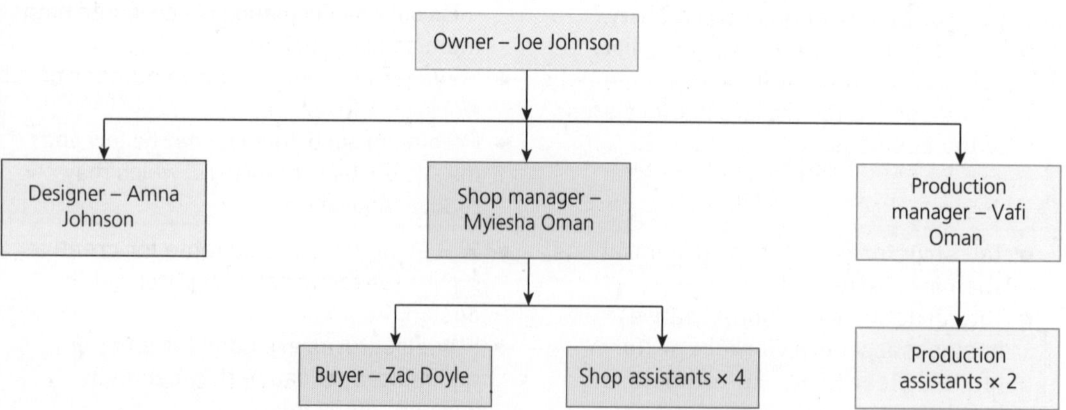

Figure 3.3 Organisation chart for J.J. Jewellery

There are five important terms connected to organisation charts that you need to know. Table 3.3 lists and explains these, and gives an example from the chart.

Table 3.3 Terminology used in organisation charts

Term	Explanation	Example from the organisation chart
Authority	The power that one person has to make decisions and to give instructions to those workers they are in charge of. A line manager is a person who is in charge of other workers.	Vafi has authority over two production assistants.
Subordinates	Workers that a line manager is responsible for.	Myiesha is a subordinate of Joe Johnson.
Delegation	A process where a manager gives a subordinate responsibility to make certain decisions, for which the manager remains ultimately responsible.	Joe Johnson has delegated responsibility for designing jewellery to Amna Johnson.
Chain of command	The link in authority from those at the top (who have most authority) to those at the bottom (who have the least).	If Joe Johnson wants to pass an instruction to the production workers, the chain of command would be from him to Vafi and then to the production workers.
Span of control	The number of subordinates that a manager has authority over.	The span of control for Joe is three – he has authority over Amna, Myiesha and Vafi.

Now test yourself

TESTED

Look again at Figure 3.2 and then answer these questions on the organisation chart for J.J. Jewellery.

1. What is the span of control of Myiesha? [1]
2. Name **one** subordinate of Joe Johnson. [1]
3. Who has Myiesha delegated authority to for buying jewellery to sell in the shop? [1]
4. If Joe Johnson wants to tell Zac Doyle to look at jewellery from a manufacturer he has heard of, what would be the chain of command? [1]
5. Who does Vafi have authority over? [1]

I can ...

- ☐ Define the terms connected with organisation charts.
- ☐ Apply the terms connected with organisation charts to specific examples.

Exam tip

A typical question on organisation charts will ask you to apply the terms. It may be followed by questions about why businesses have different organisation charts (see the next section).

Why businesses have different organisational structures

REVISED

Businesses can be organised in different ways. Compare these organisation charts with the one for J.J. Jewellery on page 42.

Figure 3.4 Organisation of a business by product and by place

When a business is organised by *product* (i.e. it makes different products, each in a different division of the business), the workers involved in the production of one product are grouped together – whether they are production, finance or marketing workers.

Another business may organise by *place* – all the workers in one geographical area are in one part of the organisation.

For J.J. Jewellery (see page 42), the workers are organised by *function* – all the production workers are together in one department, all the sales workers are in another. We have also seen (on page 41) that businesses can be organised as tall or flat structures.

There are three main reasons why businesses choose different organisation charts.

- Importance of effective communication: Communication is very important in all businesses. A business will organise its structure in a way it thinks will result in the best communications between its workers. One business may put all the workers connected with one particular product in one department so that they consider all the different but connected functions (such as marketing, production and finance) when making decisions. A business which operates in different parts of the world may organise its workers by place or area so that it is easier for them to communicate.
- Different job roles and responsibilities: A business may decide that all its workers for one function should be together so that, for example, the marketing experts are helping each other with decisions. Each function or department will focus on what it does best. It is an example of specialisation in production.
- Different ways of working: You have seen that tall and flat organisation structures suit different types of businesses. Tall organisations suit large businesses where the success depends on workers carrying out clearly defined tasks. Flat organisations are better for businesses that need their workers to be creative – a flat structure will enable workers to communicate with a range of different workers and to share ideas.

Now test yourself

TESTED ☐

1 Which of these statements about organisation structures of businesses is false? [1]

(a) An organisation structure makes it easier to communicate in a business.

(b) All organisation structures are tall.

(c) An organisation shows the different roles and responsibilities of workers in a business.

(d) Different businesses suit different types of organisation structure.

2 Coca-Cola is organised into different geographical regions. For example, there is a Middle East and North Africa Group, a Western Europe Group, a Central and Eastern Europe Group and a West Africa Unit. Coca-Cola is produced from flavouring ingredients provided by the parent company in the USA and uses local factories, people, water (its biggest ingredient) and other ingredients from the region in which it is sold. Each group is responsible for producing and bottling Coca-Cola in their region.

Analyse why it is appropriate for Coca-Cola to be organised into different geographical regions. [3]

Exam tip

Most questions ask you to apply what you have learnt to a case study business. Make sure that you explain clearly how what you are writing about is connected to the business in the question.

I can ...

- ☐ Describe different ways in which businesses may be organised.
- ☐ Analyse the reasons why businesses may organise in different ways

Ways of working

REVISED

Tables 3.4 and 3.5 summarise the different ways of working you need to learn and the main advantages and disadvantages of each – from the point of view of both the business and the worker. Each type is defined in the key terms on this page, so make sure you have learnt these before reading the tables.

Table 3.4 Advantages and disadvantages of different ways of working for a business

Way of working	Advantage to the business	Disadvantage to the business
Full-time working	The worker is permanently available for the business.	The business may have to pay a worker at a time when no work needs to be done.
Part-time working	The worker can be asked to work at specific times needed by the business.	The business may have to train many more workers than if it employed only full-time workers.
Flexible working	The business may benefit from motivated workers who like the flexibility of when they will work.	The worker may not be available to work when needed by the business.
Temporary working	The business only needs to employ workers for the length of time they need them, for example, at harvesting time.	The business may find it difficult to recruit enough workers at times when they are needed.
Working from home	The business may save costs by not having to provide office space.	Workers may not communicate with each other very well, reducing their efficiency.
Working while mobile	The business benefits from the increased productivity of the worker.	The business may not be able to monitor that the worker is working as much as he or she should.
Self-employment	Businesses often like to use self-employed contractors to do work for them because they only need them for a specific job and they do not need to pay national insurance or pension contributions for them, or to pay them when there is no work to be done.	The self-employed person may not work in the way that the business' own employees are trained to.

Flexible working: The practice of people working partly at their place of work and partly elsewhere, perhaps at home or while mobile, and possibly at times that suit them.

Full-time working: When a person works 35 hours or more per week.

Part-time working: When a person works fewer than 35 hours per week.

Self-employment: When people work in their own business, selling their work to buyers who may be consumers or other businesses.

Temporary working: When a person only works for a short period of time for an employer, sometimes on a short-term contract or sometimes on a day-to-day basis.

Working from home: When a person completes work for a business (or themselves if they are self-employed) in their home.

Working while mobile: When people work while they are on the move, travelling or on holiday.

Table 3.5 Advantages and disadvantages of different ways of working for a worker

Way of working	Advantage to the worker	Disadvantage to the worker
Full-time working	The worker is paid for a full working week.	The worker is tied to working a full working week throughout the year (except for holiday periods).
Part-time working	The worker can work when it suits them, for example, during the hours their children are in school.	The worker will only get paid for the hours they work and this may mean less money than they need or want. The worker may have to take a second job.
Flexible working	The worker can work at times that suits them, for example, they can work four long days and take the fifth day off as flexi-time.	The worker may not be offered as much work as they want.
Temporary working	The worker can work and earn for a period and then have time to do other things they want to, such as going on long holidays.	The worker may find there are times of the year when there is no work for them.
Working from home	The worker saves time and money by not having to travel to work.	The worker may find there are distractions at home such as noisy children or they may miss socialising with other workers.
Working while mobile	The worker can make full use of their time, even when they are travelling.	The worker may feel under pressure to work a lot, even while on holiday.
Self-employment	The worker may like being in control and may be highly motivated because their earnings depend on how much they produce.	There is less job security for the worker as there may be times when there is no work and so no income.

Now test yourself

TESTED ☐

Most of McDonald's' restaurant workers work on a part-time basis. They may work the same regular hours each week, for example, during a lunch period and then returning for an evening shift.

1 Analyse **one** advantage to McDonald's of employing workers on a part-time basis. [3]
2 Analyse **one** advantage to the worker of being employed by McDonald's on a part-time basis. [3]

Bolton Gates sells its products in all areas of the UK. The company sells doors and shutters for use in commercial premises such as shops and factories. John Chilton is a sales representative for Bolton Gates, and is responsible for visiting prospective customers in the Midlands. He lives in Solihull, not far from Birmingham, which is where he sells a lot of products. Some days he will visit up to four customers, on others he may have no visits to make but instead may spend time on the telephone contacting customers or writing reports to the business about the visits he makes. He mainly works from home.

3 Evaluate the possible benefits and problems for Bolton Gates of John Chilton working from home. [9]

I can ...

- ☐ Explain different ways of working.
- ☐ Analyse the advantages of different ways of working to the business and to the worker.
- ☐ Analyse the disadvantages of different ways of working to the business and to the worker.
- ☐ Evaluate whether one way of working is suitable for a business or a worker.

Exam tip

These revision notes give one key advantage and one key disadvantage to businesses and to workers of the different ways of working. This will be enough for most questions. If you are interested in finding out more, refer to the Hodder textbook OCR GCSE (9–1) Business.

3.3 Communication in business

Ways of communicating in a business context

REVISED

Table 3.6 Advantages and disadvantages of methods of communication

Method of communication	Advantages	Disadvantages
Verbal/spoken		
Phone – communication using a mobile phone or a landline.	• Good for discussion of ideas or problems and making arrangements. • It is immediate, providing the communicators are available to speak.	• No record of the discussion (unless it is recorded). • Can be difficult with long waiting times to get through to a call centre.
Meeting – people come together to have a discussion, either in person or through video-conferencing.	• It is a good way to exchange ideas and to check understanding. • Minutes (a written summary) provide a record of the meeting.	• Can be expensive to get people together. • If it is a formal meeting, it can take time to arrange.
Presentation – a speaker explains something, often using projected slides or real objects.	• The speaker has time to prepare in advance what they wish to say and then to explain clearly. • It is often possible to ask questions to help understanding.	• There may be a lot of listeners and it may be difficult to check they all understand. • Presentations take time to arrange and can be expensive.
Non-verbal/written		
Letter – a written document that is usually sent through the post.	• Provides a record of the communication. • The sender can take time to make sure ideas are clearly expressed while the reader can read the message more than once.	• It takes time for letters sent in the post to be delivered. • If the meaning of the message is unclear, it is difficult for the receiver to check.
Email – an electronic message that can be sent to an individual, a group or many people (known as 'bulkemails').	• A very fast method of communicating. • Good for short messages although attachments are a way of adding more information.	• A person may not check their emails regularly. • Bulk emails are often ignored and deleted or lost in spam.
Text – a written message sent from one phone to another. Texts can be to individuals, groups or to many people (bulk texts).	• A very fast method of communicating that can include a lot of people. • The receiver can save the text to remember details in the message, for example, of an appointment.	• Only limited information can be given. • Not good for discussing ideas.
Social media – a message sent through sites such as Facebook and Twitter.	• The message can be sent to selected groups or in bulk to large numbers cheaply. • Sometimes pictures can be added to the message.	• Somebody in the business needs to manage the communications, for example, responses from receivers. • It is not always easy to judge how successful the message has been.
Website – a business can post information on a website or let customers order on it.	• It saves money because information does not need to be printed and posted. • Customers can order online so the business may not need to have a shop or office accessible to customers.	• Customers cannot ask for information easily (unless a 'chat' facility is available). • Customers cannot view the goods.

Table 3.6 summarises the main ways of communicating that you need to know: **verbal communication** and **written communication**. Two advantages and two disadvantages are given for each **communication** method.

Communication: The transmission of a message from a sender to a receiver through a means of communication.

Verbal communication: Communicating by speaking – in meetings, by telephone, by video-**conferencing or through a presentation.**

Written communication: Communication by written words – text, email and letters.

Now test yourself

TESTED

For each of the situations below, recommend an appropriate way of communicating. Give a reason for your recommendation.

1. Next plc wants to inform its customers of what it sells and make it possible for customers to buy clothes from the comfort of their home. [3]
2. The human resources manager of LV, an insurance company, wishes to discuss with a member of staff how well he is working and to set targets for the year. [3]
3. The leader of a double glazing sales team wants to inform members of her team that their meeting will start at 4.30 p.m. and not at 4 p.m. as first announced. It is 9 a.m. on the day of the meeting. [3]

Exam tip

Questions will often ask you to recommend a way of communicating that should be used in a situation. You need to state the method you recommend and then explain clearly why it makes sense to use that method.

I can ...

- ☐ State the main verbal and non-verbal ways of communicating in business.
- ☐ Recommend the best method of communication to use for different situations.

Importance of business communications

REVISED

Good communication and **feedback** is very important in business. Communication can be internal (between people working in the same business) or external (between the business and outsiders such as customers and suppliers). Figure 3.5 shows some of the types of communication used in different business divisions.

Feedback: The response made by the person who received a communication which indicates whether they have understood the communication.

Importance of communication

Marketing communication
- Research needs to be done to find out what customers want.
- Communication is important for telling customers about the goods and services.
- The sales team may need to communicate with each other about selling the product.

Communications about human resources
- Workers need to be recruited.
- Workers need to be appraised.
- Problems between workers need to be resolved

Communications about finance
- The business may need to communicate with the bank to arrange a loan.
- Bills need to be sent out and payment recorded.
- The accounts department need information about sales and purchases to keep accurate accounts.

Communications with government
- The business will need to know the government's rules and regulations about safety and environmental regulations, for example.
- The business may ask the government for help – with money or to change rules and regulations to help it.

Business operations communications
- The production team will need to know how many goods to make.
- They will need to discuss problems about quality.

Figure 3.5 Importance of communication within different business divisions

Now test yourself

TESTED

1 The pharmacy chain, Boots, plans to increase its profits by increasing sales in its existing shops. Which of the following types of communication would Boots **not** need to use? [1]
   (a) The business would need to communicate with its market to advertise products.
   (b) Communications would be needed in human resources to plan if more workers should be recruited.
   (c) The finance department would need to communicate with business operations and marketing to find out how much finance is needed to increase sales and production.
   (d) The business would need to communicate with the government to obtain permission to increase output.

2 The Entertainer toy shop is planning a marketing campaign for the period leading up to Christmas. Analyse why communication is a very important part of this campaign. [3]

I can ...

- ☐ Explain the difference between internal and external communications.
- ☐ Give examples of how communication is used in business.
- ☐ Analyse the importance of communications to business.

Exam tip

Read the question carefully. For communications questions, think about whether the answer needs you to deal with internal or external communications, or both.

Influence of digital communication on business activity

REVISED

Email, social media, websites, mobile phones and messaging sites such as What's App and Twitter enable the **digital communication** of voice messages, video, images and text messages. The use of digital communications has changed the way many companies operate across all their business functions. Table 3.7 gives examples of the ways in which business functions have changed as a result of digital communications.

Digital communication: The electronic exchange of information using ICT.

Table 3.7 Effect of digital communications on business functions

Function	Examples of changes and their advantages or businesses and consumers
Marketing	• Businesses can sell online which means they do not need to run expensive shops or they have fewer shops or offices (e.g. banks and insurance companies). • Businesses have changed their marketing, with more emphasis now on promoting via websites and social media. • Competition has increased as it is cheaper for businesses to sell online and easier for consumers to shop around. • New business opportunities have developed such as new online TV stations and delivery services.
Human resources	• Working while mobile has become easier and is now more widely used. • Recruitment and other websites have made it easier for businesses to recruit workers. • Digital communications have increased the productivity of workers, for example, they can do more tasks (such as accounts) and do them more quickly using computers, reducing business costs.
Operations	• Production has become highly automated with the use of computer-controlled robots. Fewer workers are needed in manufacturing, reducing costs.

Now test yourself

TESTED

Blockbusters was a retail business which rented out film DVDs. Customers visited the shop to choose and rent the DVD, before returning it (usually within 24 hours or they had to pay a small fine). The development of digital communications has made it possible for companies like Netflix to offer an online film (and TV) rental service which many consumers prefer.

1 Using an example, explain the term 'digital communication in business'. [2]
2 Analyse how the way in which films are rented has changed in recent years. [3]
3 Analyse **two** ways in which digital communication has affected workers. [6]

I can ...

☐ Explain what is meant by digital communications.
☐ Analyse how digital communications have affected the different functions of business, including marketing, human resources and operations.
☐ Analyse the benefits to business of using digital communications.

Exam tip

Digital communications have greatly influenced business activity and it is likely that you will be aware of many of these through your own personal experiences. Use your own knowledge of digital communications to analyse how it is used in business. You will probably know most about how digital communications benefits customers.

3.4 Recruitment and selection

Why businesses recruit

REVISED

Recruitment refers to the process of finding people to work in a new or established business. Businesses **analyse their human resource needs** when they start up and, usually, at regular intervals once the business is established. The analysis will tell them if they need to recruit new workers to fill a **skills gap** and will identify the type of workers needed as well as how many, when and for how long. Figure 3.6 shows the main reasons why businesses need to recruit workers.

Analysing human resource needs: When an organisation decides how many and what type of workers it should employ.

Skills gap: When a business recruits skilled workers because it is short of them.

To start up a business
A business that is starting up will need workers to run it and to make the goods or provide the services it offers.

When a business grows
If a business grows it may need more workers to produce the goods or service, and more managers to oversee them.

Why businesses recruit

To replace employees who leave
Workers leave businesses for different reasons – retirement, promotion, increased pay from another business and dismissal (sacked).

To fill a skills gap
A business may be short of skilled workers either because it is growing or because it is changing the way it produces to a method which requires more skilled workers.

Figure 3.6 Why businesses recruit workers

Now test yourself

TESTED

1 Which of the following is **not** a reason why a business would recruit workers? [1]
   (a) The business intends to increase sales.
   (b) The business needs to cut costs.
   (c) The business is short of skilled workers.
   (d) Employees have retired from the business.

2 Cyber security is concerned with preventing people gaining illegal access (hacking) into computer systems. In 2016, TalkTalk, a provider of internet services, was attacked by hackers who introduced the 'Mirai worm' into its IT systems. The worm prevented customers from using the internet. In 2017, the National Health Service was attacked when hackers locked many of its computers. Cyber criminals then asked for money to unlock the computers. In the UK, there are simply not enough cyber security experts who can produce software to protect computer systems. Some organisations employ their own cyber security experts, while others employ specialist firms. As the use of ICT increases, more cyber security firms are setting up or expanding. Cyber security experts can earn a lot of money and often move from one business to another for better pay.

Analyse **two** reasons why cyber security firms need to recruit experts. [6]

Exam tip

When a question is worth six marks and asks you to do two things, each will be worth three marks.

I can ...

☐ Explain the term 'recruitment'.
☐ Analyse four reasons why businesses need to recruit workers.

Use of different recruitment methods to meet different needs

REVISED

Two documents are very important in recruitment – the **job description** and the **person specification**. The information given in these documents makes it more likely that only workers able to do a job will apply, saving time for the business and the applicants.

Business must choose whether to use **internal recruitment** or **external recruitment** when looking for a new worker. Both methods have their advantages and these are shown in Table 3.8. You can work out the disadvantages of each by thinking about the opposite of each point. For example, a disadvantage of external recruitment is that it is usually more expensive than internal recruitment.

External methods of recruitment: Includes websites, newspapers, social media and specialist magazines.

Internal methods of recruitment: Includes notice boards, word of mouth, company website and emails to staff.

Job description: A list of the main duties, tasks and responsibilities of a worker.

Person specification: A list of the qualities, qualifications and knowledge that a person should have to do a particular job.

Table 3.8 Advantages of internal and external recruitment

Advantages of internal recruitment	Advantages of external recruitment
It is cheaper to advertise internally.	It can fill a skills gap when there is no one already employed who can do the job.
Often quicker to recruit than external recruitment.	People from outside can bring new ideas.
The worker will already be known to the managers so they can be confident about the work he or she will do.	Avoids workers becoming unhappy if they are not selected but a colleague is.
The worker knows the business so there are no problems settling in.	It is necessary when the business is growing and additional workers are needed.
It can motivate workers if they see colleagues being promoted.	It saves having to recruit someone to replace a worker promoted internally.

Table 3.9 describes the media which a business can use to recruit workers. It states whether the media is suitable for internal and/or external recruitment and some gives key points to remember about each type.

Table 3.9 Recruitment media

Media	Internal or external	Key points
Website	Both	The firm's own website or a special site advertising jobs.
Social media	Both	This is now widely used as many potential applicants use social media.
Local newspapers	External	Appropriate when the job is likely to appeal only to people who live near the business.
National newspapers	External	Appropriate when workers from a very wide geographical area may apply, but advertising in them is expensive.
Specialist magazines and journals	External	Good for recruiting workers such as engineers, doctors and HR specialists who read journals and magazines relevant to their particularly job expertise.
Job centre	External	These are run by the government and give workers the opportunity to use computers and find out about a wide range of jobs.

Media	Internal or external	Key points
Word of mouth	Both	Existing employees tell friends and others about jobs, which saves the business money.
Email	Internal	The business can send an advertisement to workers they know may be interested in the job.
Noticeboard or company magazine	Internal	This is cheap and will be seen by workers likely to be interested in the job.

Job advertisements need to include enough detail to attract the right kind of person to apply, for example, contact information (business address and phone number/email address), details about the job (some information from the job description), details about the person needed (some information from the person specification), pay and conditions.

Now test yourself

TESTED

Aldi is opening a new supermarket in Stoke. It needs to recruit:

- an experienced shop manager to get the supermarket off to a good start
- 20 shop assistants to work in the store.

Recommend how you would recruit these workers. Give reasons for your recommendations. [6]

Exam tip

Use the information in the table about the advantages of internal and external recruitment when recommending which recruitment method to use. Think about the types of workers needed, the numbers needed, where the work is and how much money the business can afford to spend on recruitment. The key is to justify any recommendation you make.

I can ...

- ☐ Explain what is meant by internal and external recruitment.
- ☐ Explain the terms 'job description' and 'person specification' and why these are useful when recruiting workers.
- ☐ Analyse when to use internal or external recruitment.
- ☐ Recommend the media to use when recruiting workers.
- ☐ Explain what should be included in a job advertisement.

Methods of selection

REVISED

Businesses need to obtain information about the people who apply for a job. They use this information to decide which of the applicants will be best be able to do the job.

Figure 3.7 gives the main points about each of the methods of **selection** a business can use.

Selection: The process of choosing between applicants for a job.

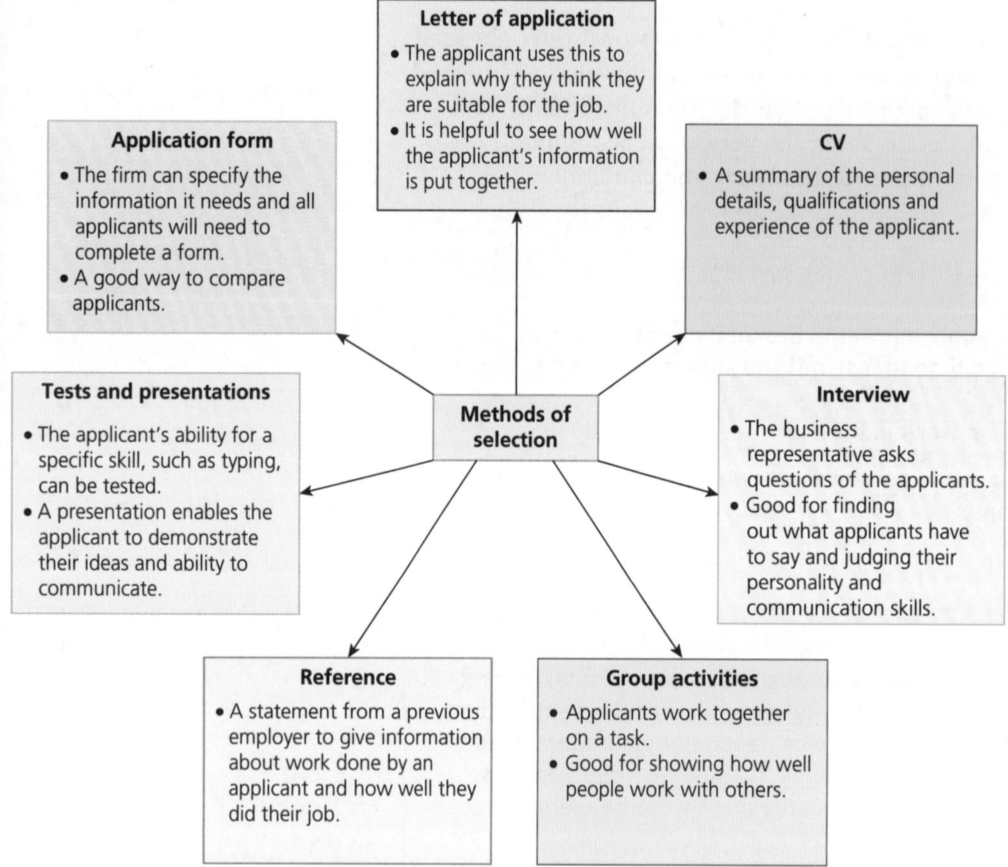

Figure 3.7 Methods of selecting a job applicant

Now test yourself

TESTED

Aldi is opening a new supermarket in Stoke. It needs to recruit an experienced shop manager to get the supermarket off to a good start. The HR manager has used information from letters of application and CVs to choose five candidates to go to the final stage of selection. The HR manager needs to choose two methods of selection to use to decide which of the five applicants to employ.

Recommend **two** methods of selection that Aldi should use to decide which of the five applicants to employ. [6]

Exam tip

Make sure you are clear about the job the worker will do and the skills and qualifications needed. You should be able to analyse how the different methods of selection will provide the information the business needs.

I can ...

- ☐ Explain the different methods of selection.
- ☐ Recommend when a business should make use of each of the different methods of selection.

3.5 Motivation and retention

Financial methods of motivation

REVISED

Workers who feel safe at work, who feel that their contribution to the organisation is valued and that their talents are recognised and encouraged are likely to feel motivated. Successful organisations ensure they motivate their workers.

Financial methods of **motivation** (see Figure 3.8) all involve some kind of payment, either in money or in kind (i.e. free goods and/or services) to encourage workers to work longer or more efficiently.

Bonus: An additional payment to workers for achieving a target.

Fringe benefits: Additional benefits that workers may receive in addition to their pay, such as health insurance, gym membership and childcare vouchers.

Motivation: Encouragement given to workers to work well.

Pay: The money earned by workers as a reward for the work they do.

Profit sharing: When workers receive some of the profits made by a business.

Financial methods of motivation

Pay (wage or salary)

- A wage is usually paid weekly and is based on the number of hours worked. An extra amount per hour can be paid for overtime or unsociable hours. It motivates workers because the more they work the more they earn.
- A problem is that a wage does not reward workers for how well they work, only how long.
- A salary is an annual sum divided into 12 monthly payments. A salary is often paid to professional workers such as teachers, accountants, HR managers.
- It motivates workers as they receive a regular income.

Bonus

- A payment that a worker receives in addition to their pay, usually for meeting a production or sales target. A bonus is often paid to individuals or teams whose output can be measured.
- It motivates workers because the more they produce or sell, the more they earn. It improves their productivity.
- Targets need to be fair and realistic or workers will not feel motivated.

Profit sharing

- Workers are paid a part of the profits of the business.
- A profit share may be paid to workers whose individual output cannot be measured.
- It motivates them because they know if they work efficiently, the business will make more profit and it will increase their income.
- A drawback is that it reduces the profits for shareholders.

Fringe-benefit

- These are benefits in kind given to workers on top of their pay, such as free health insurance.
- They motivate workers because they provide them with an attractive package of pay and benefits. They can be good for motivating workers not to leave a business.
- Fringe benefits are a cost to a business so may reduce profits.

Figure 3.8 Financial methods of motivation

Exam tip

Be sure you can recommend which type of financial method of motivation is appropriate for a particular type of worker. Be ready to justify (explain) your answer.

Now test yourself

TESTED

A farm employs workers to pick cabbages during the harvest period. Which method of financial motivation would motivate the workers to pick as many cabbages in a day as they could? [1]

(a) A weekly wage.
(b) A bonus system.
(c) Fringe benefits such as free health insurance.
(d) A salary.

I can ...

- ☐ Explain what motivation means.
- ☐ Explain what financial motivation is.
- ☐ Explain the methods of financial motivation.
- ☐ Describe the types of workers who will be motivated by different methods of financial motivation.

Non-financial methods of motivation

REVISED

Non-financial methods of motivation (see Table 3.10) are ways of encouraging workers to work longer or more efficiently but which do not involve paying them extra money for example, by **praise**, an **award scheme** or providing a good **working environment**.

Award scheme: A presentation to recognise an individual worker or team's effort and achievement.

Table 3.10 Non-financial methods of motivation

Method	Praise	Award scheme	Working environment
Description	Workers are thanked and praised for the (good) work they have done, either in private or publicly in front of other workers.	Workers are presented with rewards for their work. These might include vouchers for days out, holidays or simply certificates of achievement.	Improving the workplace so that it is a pleasant place to work. It can also involve listening to people and giving them a say in the business or sending them on team building activities.
How it motivates	It makes workers feel appreciated and valued. Those not praised may feel that they need to do better to earn praise.	Makes workers feel valued and will encourage them and others to continue to increase their efforts.	Makes workers feel well looked after and that their opinions are valued.
Advantage	It does not cost the business anything and it helps to create a positive climate.	Cost of these rewards varies but not all are expensive to give.	If workers feel valued they will respect the business and their colleagues, creating a positive attitude to work.
Disadvantage	Sometimes if there is no financial reward for good work over a long period, workers may feel that they are not truly valued.	There is some cost to them. They need to be given fairly or workers who do not receive an award may be upset.	There is a cost to some of this, for example, improving the furniture or facilities in a building or paying for activities.
Suitable for	All workers as everyone likes to feel appreciated.	All workers as everyone likes to feel appreciated.	Most workers, except for those who work in conditions where improvements to comfort are difficult, such as those working on a North Sea oil rig or in a mine.

Now test yourself

TESTED

Herefordshire Care Homes uses non-financial methods of motivation for the care assistants who look after the elderly people who live in its homes. Employees can be nominated for awards by a colleague. The awards include:

- a certificate and letter of recognition
- a gift
- a brief article about the worker on the company website.

1 Analyse **one** advantage of this scheme. [3]
2 Analyse **one** disadvantage of this scheme. [3]

Praise: A way of motivating a worker by complimenting their work and so making them feel recognised and valued.

Working environment: The quality of the physical workplace and its atmosphere (how people treat each other, etc.)

I can ...

☐ Explain what non-financial motivation is.
☐ Explain the methods of non-financial motivation.
☐ Recommend the types of workers who will be motivated by different methods of non-financial motivation.

Exam tip

Be sure you can recommend which type of non-financial method of motivation is appropriate for each type of worker. Be ready to justify (explain) your answer.

Now test yourself answers at www.hoddereducation.co.uk/myrevisionnotesdownloads

Importance of employee motivation and Importance of employee retention

REVISED

Motivated workers will reduce costs and increase sales, through improved employee performance. Table 3.11 explains why motivated workers help businesses to compete, survive and grow.

Table 3.11 Benefits of motivated workers

Benefit	Explanation
High worker productivity	Workers will produce more goods or improved services in the time they work. This will reduce the costs of production and the prices the business charges can be reduced so that sales and profits rise.
Reduced levels of worker supervision	Workers will want to do their job well. This may reduce business costs as fewer supervisors need to be employed.
Low worker absenteeism	Workers will be happy about coming into work and less likely to take a day off if they are only slightly unwell.
Improved quality	Workers will take pride in doing their work well and will produce quality goods and services, knowing that this will satisfy consumers and give the business a good name. There will be less waste which helps to reduce costs.

A high employee **retention** means workers stay with a business for a long period of time. A low employee retention rate means that workers do not stay long and there is a high **labour turnover**.

Workers will be happy to stay with a business if they feel they are being treated fairly. For example, they will feel that their pay is what they deserve, that they are respected by their managers and that there are opportunities in the business for them to develop their skills and make progress in their careers.

Benefits of workers staying a long period of time:

- The business will need to recruit workers less often, saving time and recruitment costs.
- Training costs will be lower because the business will not need to train as many new workers. Workers will already be familiar with the business and its customers, so will need less training.
- When the firm does want to recruit new workers, it will be easier for them to do so because it will have a good reputation for treating its workers well.

However, not all businesses want to retain their workers for a long period of time. Sometimes workers may only needed for a particular length of time, for example, a hotel may require more workers during the summer tourist season and shops may take on extra staff for the Christmas period.

Labour turnover: A measure of the number or proportion of staff who leave an organisation each year and who therefore need to be replaced.

Motivation: How workers are encouraged to work well.

Retention: When workers choose to stay employed in a business rather than leaving to work elsewhere.

Now test yourself

TESTED

Blossom Farm grows a range of vegetables. These are harvested during the months of August and September and during this period, farm labourers are needed to work in the fields doing hard manual work such as bending down to cut cabbages from their stems.

Belle Hair is a chain of hairdressing salons with shops in several towns. It has a good reputation and many of its customers are regulars. It employs 76 workers, most of whom are hairdressers.

1 Evaluate why the retention of workers is likely to be more important for Belle Hair than it is for Blossom Farm. [9]
2 Recommend **one** way in which Blossom Farm could motivate the farm labourers it employs.
Give a reason for your recommendation. [3]
3 Recommend **one** way in which Belle Hair could motivate the hairdressers it employs. Give a reason for your recommendation. [3]

Exam tip

With 'recommend' questions there may be more than one possible answer. While your recommendation needs to be appropriate, the key to gaining further marks will be how well you justify your recommendation.

I can ...

- ☐ Analyse the importance of motivation to a business.
- ☐ Evaluate when to use different methods of motivation.
- ☐ Explain the meaning of retention.
- ☐ Analyse the importance of retention to a business.
- ☐ Evaluate when high retention is good for a business and when it is not necessary.

3.6 Training and development

Different training methods

REVISED

Training involves developing a worker's specific skills, for example, by teaching them to operate the company computer system, deal with customers or work safely. **Induction** training occurs when a worker first joins a company. Training is divided into on-the-job and off-the-job.

On-the-job training usually involves a trainee working with a more experienced worker who shows the trainee what to do and then gives them feedback to improve their skills as they do their work. Somebody learning to ice a cake might learn in this way. Table 3.12 describes the advantages and disadvantages of on-the-job training.

Induction: Training to introduce a new worker to an organisation, including how to do the job, how it fits within the operation of the business and an introduction to others in the organisation.

Table 3.12 Advantages and disadvantages of on-the-job training

Advantages of on-the-job training	Disadvantages of on-the-job training
It is specific to the individual and the business.	The work done as the learner starts to train may not be of a good enough quality.
It saves on the cost of travel to a course.	The trainer may be good at their job but not at training others how to do it.
The worker produces something as he or she trains.	The worker may learn only how to do the work in the way the business does it.
The business can teach the person exactly how they want the job done.	The worker may not obtain a qualification as a result of the training.
	It is not easy to train a group of trainees.

Off-the-job training is when the worker is away from his or her work. Figure 3.9 shows the different types of off-the-job training while Table 3.13 shows the advantages and disadvantages.

Off-the-job training: Occurs away from the job. It may still be at the place of work or the employee may be sent elsewhere for training.

On-the-job training: Occurs at the place of work and while the worker is doing his or her job.

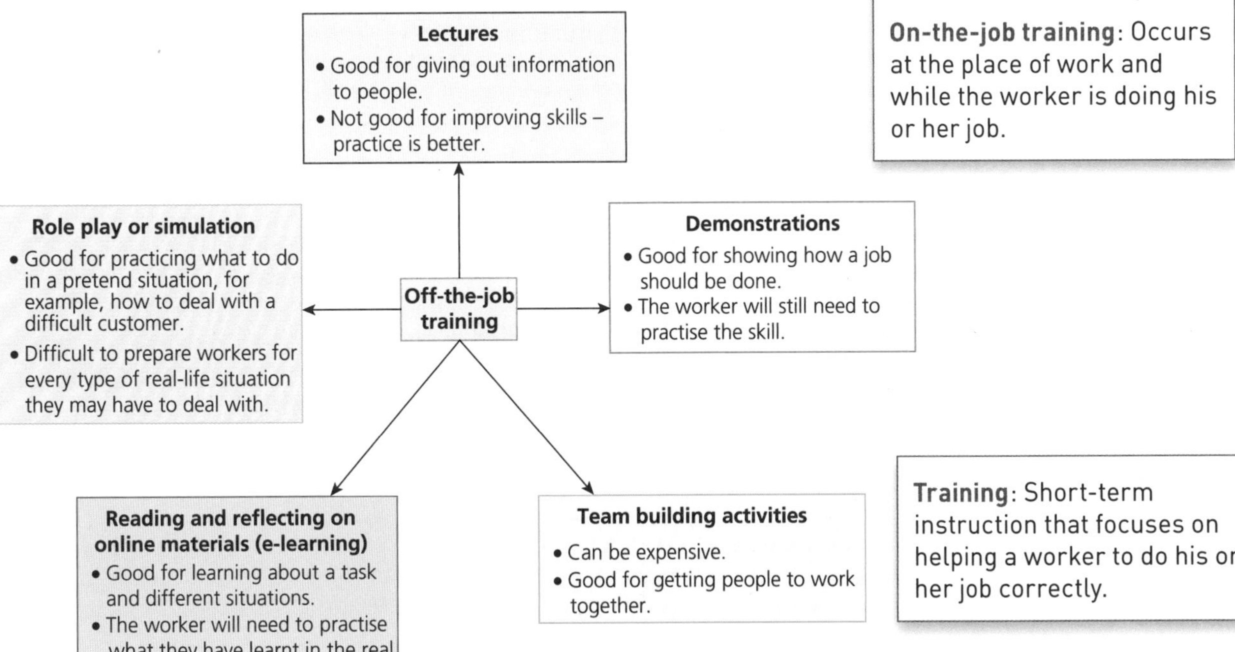

Figure 3.9 Types of off-the-job training

Training: Short-term instruction that focuses on helping a worker to do his or her job correctly.

Table 3.13 Advantages and disadvantages of off-the-job training

Advantages of off-the-job training	Disadvantages of off-the-job training
Training is often given by experts.	It can be expensive – the employer will have to pay travel costs and training fees.
The trainee may be motivated by a day away from work.	The business loses output while the worker is away from work.
A worker can feel valued because the business is paying for the training.	Improving a worker's skills may make it possible for them to get work in another business.
Some types of training, e.g. safety, are better carried out by experts.	

The training a worker receives when they first start working at a business is known as induction training and can be either on- or off-the-job training. An advantage of induction training is that the worker will more quickly get to know their co-workers and better understand their role and the business as a whole. A disadvantage to the business is that the worker's wages, and the wages of the person training them, will be paid even though they are not producing anything during the induction period.

Now test yourself

TESTED

1 A health clinic wishes to begin offering acupuncture to its patients. Acupuncture involves inserting fine needles into the patient. The clinic needs to train one of its physiotherapists how to do this. Recommend whether on-the-job or off-the-job training should be used. [3]

2 A garage wishes to train an apprentice mechanic. The firm employs several fully-trained, highly-skilled mechanics. Analyse **one** advantage and **one** disadvantage to the business of using on-the-job training for this. [6]

Exam tip

Questions will either be about on- or off-the-job training or about how off-the-job training is done. Be ready to discuss how the advantages and disadvantages of each apply to a specific training situation.

I can ...

- ☐ Explain the meaning of on- and off-the-job training, and induction training.
- ☐ Apply the advantages and disadvantages of on-the-job training to an example training need.
- ☐ Apply the advantages and disadvantages of off-the-job training to an example training need.
- ☐ Recommend the type of training appropriate for different situations.

Why businesses train their workers

REVISED

Reasons why a business trains its workers:

- Introduces new recruits to the business and their work (induction training).
- Gives workers technical skills such as how to use a fork-lift truck.
- Develops workers' personal skills such as leadership, communication and organisation.
- Inform workers of health and safety procedures.
- Inform workers about employment law or rules such as discrimination in the workplace.
- Teach workers to manage others.
- Teach workers to function together as a group.
- Tell workers about the features of new products that they will be selling.
- Train workers to be flexible so that they can do different types of jobs as needed.
- Teach workers new skills if their existing skills are no longer needed.

Benefits to a business of training its workers:

- Improves workers' **productivity** and so it reduces the business' production costs.
- Improves the quality of goods or services (including customer service) offered by the business, increasing its sales, revenue and profits.
- Helps the growth and development of the business.
- Solves skill shortages by training up existing staff.
- May improve motivation and retention.
- Ensures that goods and services are produced safely.

Productivity: A measure of output per worker, which can be used to measure the performance of a worker.

Now test yourself

TESTED

1 A business has recruited ten new workers. Which of the following will **not** be a reason for training these workers? [1]
   (a) To introduce them to other workers and show them around the premises.
   (b) To tell them about health and safety in the business.
   (c) To help them to move on to other companies.
   (d) To teach them the skills needed to do their jobs.

2 Homebase, the DIY store, sends sales assistants who work in the gardening sections of its shops on a garden licence training scheme. The course takes a year and is accredited by City & Guilds.

Analyse **two** benefits that Homebase may gain by sending workers on the garden licence training scheme. [6]

Exam tip

When writing about why businesses train their workers, think about the skills a trainee will learn and how this will benefit the business.

I can ...

- ☐ List the reasons why workers train their workers.
- ☐ Explain and apply the benefits businesses gain from training their workers.

Staff development

REVISED

Staff development involves learning over a long period of time. Workers may learn through an external course, with learning being reinforced by practical activity in the workplace. The aim is to realise the long-term potential of the employee. Workers can gain vocational qualifications (which are specific to a job) or academic qualifications (which are more theoretical).

Two types of staff development are compared in Table 3.14. In practice, they are not quite so different as apprentices may experience professional development at the same time they complete their **apprenticeship**, or they may progress to a **professional development** programme.

Apprenticeship: A long-term development programme for workers to learn job skills while they work.

Professional development: Involves developing the long-term potential of workers.

Staff development: Includes apprenticeships and professional development programmes.

Table 3.14 Comparison of two types of staff development

Apprenticeship	Professional development programme
A long-term learning programme – often over two, three or four years.	A long-term programme – often two years or more.
Usually leads to a specific National Vocational Qualification (NVQ), for example, Level 2 qualification in childcare or a Level 3 qualification in plumbing.	May lead to a professional qualification such as a Chartered Surveyor or a member of the Association of Dental Anaesthetists. It may lead to general academic qualifications such as a degree.
It develops skills and knowledge relevant to a specific job, e.g. veterinary nursing.	It contributes to a person's general education as well as enabling them to develop a set of skills and body of knowledge related to a specific vocation, such as medicine, business management or accountancy.
Available at two main levels – intermediate (for people with GCSEs) and advanced (for people with GCSEs and A levels). Some apprenticeships go on to degree-level work and beyond.	Professional development applies at all levels from junior to senior workers.
The development programme is usually completed partly in the work place and partly in a college.	Professional development programmes often include a high academic content completed at college or online, but there will also be a practical element.

Now test yourself

TESTED

The White Horse Inn has trained several apprentice chefs in recent years. Ryan Bollard was an apprentice at the Inn. He worked with the chef to learn to produce a range of meals and during this time he gained a Level 2 and a Level 3 NVQ. Ryan went on to study for a degree in hospitality management. Now he is the Operations Manager for the business.

1 Analyse how Ryan's experience was typical of an apprenticeship. [3]
2 Explain **two** features of a professional development programme. [4]

I can ...

- ☐ Explain the meaning of the term 'staff development'.
- ☐ Explain the difference between vocational and academic qualifications.
- ☐ Explain how an apprenticeship is an example of staff development.
- ☐ Explain how professional development is as an example of staff development.

Exam tip

If the question asks about staff development in general you can use information about either apprenticeships and/or professional development programmes.

Benefits to employees and businesses of staff development

REVISED

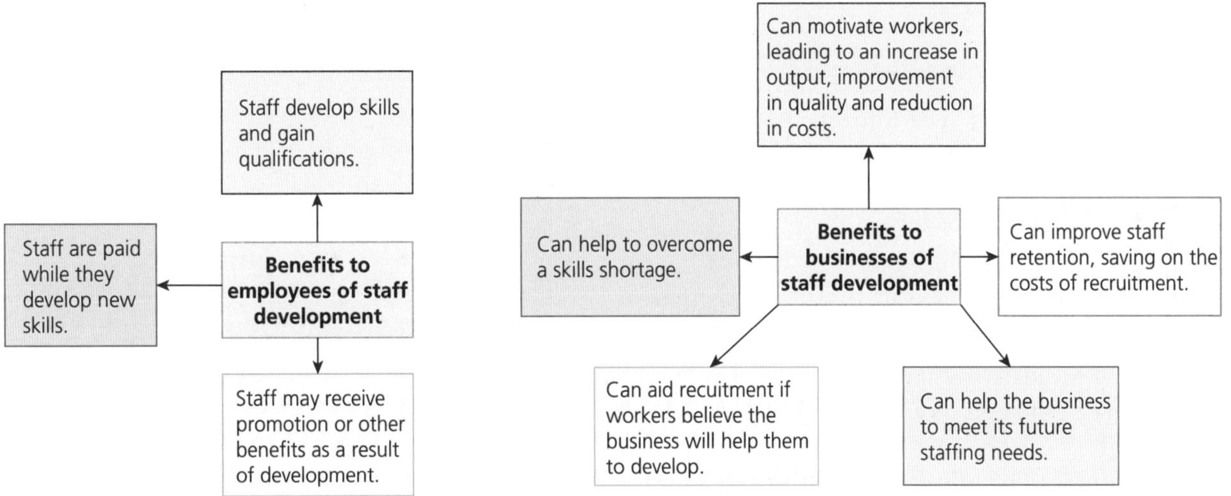

Figure 3.10 Benefits of staff development to businesses and employees

Figure 3.10 describes the benefits of staff development to both the business and the employees. However, there may be problems for the business resulting from staff development, as outlined below.

- Staff development costs money, so when a business is experiencing a decrease in its profits or a financial loss, it may decide to reduce staff development costs as a way of increasing profits or even of staying in business.
- Staff who have completed their training may find that they can get a better job elsewhere.

Now test yourself

TESTED

Of the 20 people who work at Holts Jewellery, 9 started with the business as an apprentice. The business found that when experienced jewellers retired there were not enough skilled people to replace them, so it started to train its own apprentices in jewellery design and manufacturing, including skills such as pearl stringing, lapidary (engraving, cutting and polishing stones and gems) and goldsmithing. Holts Jewellery now has expert jewellers which it believes sets it apart from many other jewellery businesses.

Evaluate the benefits to Holts Jewellery of its apprenticeship scheme. [9]

I can ...

- ☐ Explain the benefits of staff development for employees.
- ☐ Explain the benefits of staff development for business.
- ☐ Explain the costs of staff development for businesses.
- ☐ Evaluate the usefulness of staff development for a business.

Exam tip

When answering 'evaluate' questions, write about the advantages and disadvantages of the given scenario, then try to come to an overall conclusion. Use evidence from the case study as well as from what you know of the real world of business, or say what information you would need to make a judgement.

3.7 Employment law

Impact of current legislation on recruitment and employment

REVISED

Discrimination laws

Discrimination is illegal. The Equality Act 2010 says a person cannot be treated differently on the grounds of their gender, race, ethnicity, disability, sexual orientation (LGBT – lesbian, gay, bisexual and transgender), religion or beliefs.

A business must not:

- pay workers differently for doing the same work
- favour certain types of people when recruiting workers, for example, advertising for male workers (unless an exception in law has been made)
- discriminate when promoting or training workers or making then redundant
- allow workers to be mistreated by other workers because of, for example, their skin colour, sexual orientation or religion.

A business that does discriminate may find:

- staff become less motivated, which may affect the performance of the business
- workers decide to leave, so the business must recruit workers
- it develops a poor reputation, which could reduce sales and affect recruitment
- it can be fined and made to pay compensation to employees.

A business that takes action to stop discrimination may find:

- it increases costs, for example, it may have to raise the pay for women
- it needs to rewrite recruitment and training policies to prevent discrimination
- it needs to monitor what goes on in the business to prevent discrimination taking place.

Contract of employment

A **contract of employment** makes clear what the worker is being employed to do and the pay and conditions that the business will give to the worker, including holiday entitlement. A **statement of employment particulars** is a written part of a contract of employment which gives details of pay, conditions and holiday entitlement. It must be given to the worker within eight weeks of starting work.

Contract of employment: A legal agreement between an employer and an employee.

Discrimination: Treating one worker differently to another for no acceptable reason.

Employment law: Regulations and rules put in place to protect workers from employers who may treat them unfairly.

Statement of employment particulars: Part of a contract of employment, it gives details of the terms of employment.

All workers are entitled to holidays each year, depending on how many hours per week they work for the business. Normally, workers cannot be asked to work more than 48 hours per week, though there are some exceptions (e.g. police officers, people in the armed forces, seamen and servants in private households), but workers can opt out of this legal restriction if they wish to.

The effects of providing a contract of employment to all workers include:

- increased costs because the business may need to employ additional people to cover workers who are on holiday or who can only work a limited number of hours each week
- managing staff holidays to ensure there are always enough workers to do the work.

Now test yourself

TESTED ☐

1 Analyse **two** problems that a business may face if it discriminates against an employee. [6]

2 Analyse the benefit of a contract of employment to:
  (a) the business
  (b) a worker. [6]

Exam tip

When revising this topic, make sure you understand what is meant by discrimination and what a contract of employment is, but focus on the effect of these on a business.

I can ...

- ☐ Explain what is meant by discrimination in recruitment and employment.
- ☐ Analyse the impact on business of laws which are designed to stop discrimination.
- ☐ Explain what a contract of employment and a statement of employment particulars are.
- ☐ Analyse the impact on a business of contracts of employment.

4 Operations

4.1 Production processes

Different production processes and their impact on businesses

REVISED

Businesses can use **job**, **batch** or **flow production** to manufacture goods. You need to be able to discuss the *impact* of these types of **production processes** on a business, both in terms of the positive impacts (advantages) and the possible negative impacts (disadvantages) (see Table 4.1).

Batch production: A method of production where one type of product is made and then production is switched to make a different product.

Flow production: Production of one product that takes place continuously using a production assembly line. It is sometimes called mass production.

Job production: A method of production where products are made individually.

Production processes: The three methods or processes of production – job, batch and flow.

Table 4.1 Advantages and disadvantages of three types of production processes

Method of production	Advantages	Disadvantages
Job production, e.g. a bridge, piece of artwork, item of furniture, hand-made item of clothing.	• The item is likely to be of a high quality and is a one-off, bespoke item (i.e. designed to meet the individual needs of the customer). • The business can often charge a high price and make a good profit.	• Can be a high cost method of production, especially if it requires especially skilled workers to produce the item. • Production may be slow and the customer may have to wait for the product.
Batch production, e.g. loaves of bread, paint.	• Batches can be varied to meet the needs of different customers. • There are no storage costs if goods are made to order. • It is cheaper than job production.	• Machines need re-setting between different batches, which costs money. • Stocks of raw materials may be needed – extra costs. • Tasks may be repetitive and boring for workers, leading to motivation and staff retention problems.
Flow production, e.g. motor car assembly	• Large quantities are produced for sale. • The business may gain economies of large-scale production which can reduce unit costs. • Use of machinery/automation can reduce costs. • Use of computer controlled machinery allows some variation in products.	• Mass-produced goods may not be of high quality. • The business may need to store large stocks of materials ready for use on the production line. • Production can be disrupted, for example, by a mechanical break-down. • Tasks may be repetitive and boring for workers, leading to motivation and staff retention problems.

Now test yourself

TESTED

Cadbury's has enough demand for its chocolate bars to be able to manufacture them using flow production. This means the chocolate bars are produced continuously on a production line. Cadbury's does not use batch production, which would involve making one type of bar and then switching to another type of chocolate bar.

1 Analyse **one** benefit to Cadbury's of producing its chocolate bars using flow production. [3]
2 Analyse **one** possible problem to Cadbury's of producing its chocolate bars using flow production. [3]

Adam Ansel is a portrait photographer. He takes pictures of families and children.

3 Recommend the production process that Adam Ansel should use. [3]

Exam tip

If the question asks you to recommend the production process a business should use, think about the type of product and buyer, how much consumers are willing to pay, the importance of low costs and prices and the number of competitors the business has.

I can ...

- ☐ Explain the different types of production – job, batch and flow.
- ☐ Recommend when businesses should use each type of production.

Influence of technology on production and the impact on businesses

REVISED

Automation, **robotics** and computers are examples of how technology can be used in the production of goods and services. They are treated separately below but most questions in the exam will focus on technology in general.

Automation: A production process involving machinery that is controlled by a computer rather than a person.

Robotics: The use of robots in the production process.

Robotics
Robots are machines that are programmed to do work such as welding, tightening bolts and paint-spraying in the production of cars.

Computers
Computers can be programmed to control machines. Workers use computers to help them do their work, e.g. keeping accounts on spreadsheets, writing letters.

Use of technology in production

Automation
Machinery completes repetitive tasks without continuous input from an operator, for example:

- a machine to fill tins of paint and put lids on them
- sensors to control heating systems
- sensors used to automatically control the direction and speed of a vehicle
- a vending machine to automatically dispense food and drinks.

Figure 4.1 Use of technology in production

The impact of using technology in production is summarised in Table 4.2.

Table 4.2 Impact of using technology in production

Advantages of using technology in production	Disadvantages of using technology in production
Machines can replace workers, reducing costs.	The business may need to recruit skilled labour to program the computers which control production.
Worker productivity is increased as computers help them to work faster and produce more. This reduces costs.	Workers may need to be retrained to work with the new technology and training costs money.
Waste is reduced as machines are usually more accurate than humans.	Machines can break down, disrupting production.
Production can be flexible as machines can be programmed to change what is produced.	New technology may be expensive to buy. Customers may not like automation, for example, automated telephone response systems.
Technology can operate 24/7 and never needs time off work, again reducing costs and increasing output.	The storage of data about customers must meet the requirements of data protection laws.
Human safety is improved as machines can do dangerous jobs.	
New technology can lead to new products for businesses to sell.	

Be ready to explain that technology is being used more and more in all kinds of production because of the advantages it can bring. However, it is not always useful. For example, craft workers may still need to use their manual skills, for example, to paint or make pottery. Service workers may still need to use their manual skills, for example, hairdressers and nurses.

Now test yourself

TESTED ☐

Manchester Airport uses an automated system for handling passengers' baggage. For every flight, the system sends each customer's baggage on a conveyor belt to the gate where their plane will leave from. It is then manually transferred onto the plane by baggage handlers.

1. Analyse **one** advantage to Manchester Airport of using an automated system for handling baggage. [3]
2. Analyse **one** disadvantage to Manchester Airport of using an automated system for handling baggage. [3]

I can ...

- ☐ Explain what is meant by technology in the production process.
- ☐ Give examples of the use of technology in the production of goods and services.
- ☐ Analyse the impact (possible advantages and disadvantages) of technology on businesses.
- ☐ Evaluate when using technology will be useful and when it will not.

Exam tip

Most questions will be about the impact of technology on production. The key advantage is about reductions in costs, but remember there are several ways to explain why this happens.

4.2 Quality of goods and services

Concept of quality *and* Importance of quality in the production of goods and the provision of services

REVISED

The concept of **quality** means the good or service:

- is fit for purpose (i.e. it does what it is supposed to do)
- complies with all relevant legal requirements, for example, design and safety legislation
- does what the customer expects, for example, if the customer has paid for a high quality hotel, this is what should be provided.

Figure 4.2 summarises the key benefits of providing quality goods and services.

Quality: Refers to a product (goods or service) being fit for purpose.

Recalls: When a fault occurs with a product and the business asks for the product to be brought back so it can be repaired or replaced.

Returns: Goods which customers take back to the shop or online retailer because they are unsuitable or faulty.

Benefits of providing quality goods and services

Waste is reduced

The number of goods which are 'rejects' is reduced. This reduces:

- **recalls** of defective products
- the **return** of products from dissatisfied customers
- goods having to be sold as 'second' a lower price and profit (seconds are goods that have a minor fault)

The business gains a good reputation

Satisfied customers will:

- buy in the future from the business, so it retains customers
- recommend the business to others, so the business gains customers
- reduce the risk of the business developing a poor reputation, so it does not lose customers.

Figure 4.2 Benefits of providing quality goods and services

Now test yourself

TESTED

According to the 2006 American Customer Satisfaction Index, Papa John's does better pizza than larger rivals Pizza Hut and Domino's in a survey of the quality of pizzas and service provided in the restaurants.

'We have a fundamental belief that if you serve a superior quality pizza with excellent service and value, consumers will recognize the difference and reward you with repeat business,' said John H. Schnatter, Papa John's founder and executive chairman.

Analyse **two** possible benefits to Papa John's of having a better reputation for quality than its competitors. [6]

I can ...

- ☐ Explain what is meant by quality.
- ☐ Analyse the importance of quality in the production of goods and provision of services.

Exam tip

When evaluating the effect of poor quality, it will depend on the *extent* of the quality problems. If there is only one customer complaint, this is unlikely to greatly affect the company, but if there are lots of customer complaints, word will spread and this can lead to a reduction in sales.

Methods of ensuring quality

REVISED

Quality control usually involves a physical inspection by an inspector or by a machine to check each product is of a sufficiently high standard. For services, it may involve a mystery shopper buying a product in a shop or buying a service.

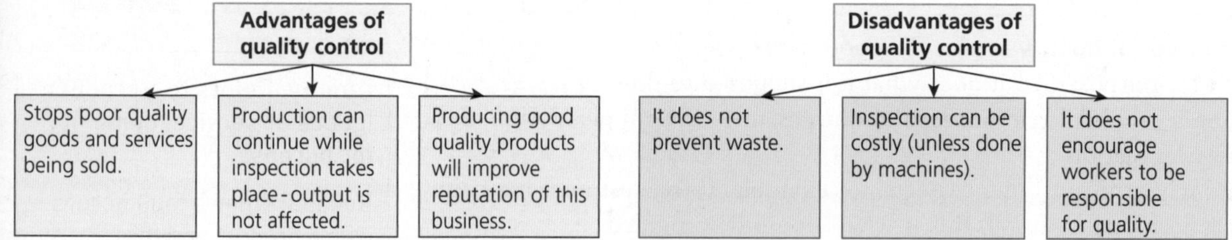

Figure 4.3 Advantages and disadvantages of quality control

A firm that uses **quality assurance** makes all its workers responsible for quality. If a worker makes something which is then used by another worker, the second worker is a 'customer' of the first who needs to be satisfied that what he or she has been given is of a high enough quality.

Table 4.3 Advantages and disadvantages of quality assurance

Advantages of quality assurance	Disadvantages of quality assurance
It should reduce wastage and costs.	Workers may be stressed by the responsibility of having to check the quality of their own work.
All workers are responsible for quality which may motivate them to take care.	
If quality goods and services result it will improve the reputation of the business.	

Quality assurance: An approach that involves the whole business focusing on quality with the aim of preventing quality problems from arising.

Quality control: A system for inspecting the quality of the goods or services produced and ensuring that they are of the required standard.

Exam tip

Be ready to distinguish between the two methods of ensuring quality. You may need to say which system is being used in a case study business. Also be ready to apply the advantages and disadvantages of the appropriate system.

Now test yourself

TESTED

The Santa Cruz Guitar company is a small company manufacturing guitars. To maintain efficiency, the shop floor is divided into six workstations in which guitars are partially assembled and then moved to the next station. Each bench is manned by a senior craft worker, and no guitar leaves a station until the craft worker is 100 per cent happy with its quality.

1 State the method of ensuring quality that is used by the Santa Cruz Guitar Company. Explain your answer. [2]
2 Analyse **one** advantage to the Santa Cruz Guitar Company of using this method of ensuring quality. [3]

I can ...

- ☐ Explain the meaning of quality control and quality assurance.
- ☐ Analyse the advantages and disadvantages of each method of ensuring quality.

4.3 Sales process and customer services

Methods of selling

REVISED

The three methods of selling that you need to know are e-commerce, **face to face** and **telesales**. These methods can be used to sell both goods and services and to sell to consumers and other businesses.

E-commerce is dealt with in detail in the next section but it refers to selling online. Face-to-face selling and telesales are dealt with in Table 4.4. The bullet points indicate the advantages and disadvantages to the customer (c) and business (b).

Face to face: Involves direct contact between buyer and seller, for example, a sale completed in a shop.

Telesales: Sales completed over the telephone.

Table 4.4 Advantages and disadvantages of different methods of selling

Method	Advantages	Disadvantages
Face-to-face selling – when the buyer and seller meet, e.g. in a shop	• Can increase sales (b). • Useful where customers like advice and personal service from assistants (c), e.g. when choosing a wedding dress or for detailed information about a holiday destination. • Can help sales in business-to-business (B2B) selling (c and b), e.g. for discussing detailed specifications of technical equipment. • For some services, it may be unavoidable, for example, restaurant meals or in door-to-door selling (c). • The customer can bargain with the seller over the price or the services (c).	• May not always be convenient for customers (c). • If the customer bargains with the seller for a better deal, profits may be reduced (b). • Retailer costs are high if expensive shops are needed (b).
Telesales – the buyer buys from a telesales worker by phone.	Can increase sales (b) as customers can ask questions about products and bargain about the price (e.g. renewing Sky TV contracts and mobile phone contracts) (c). May cost less than selling from a shop (c and b).	Costs involved such as a warehouse to store goods and payment to telesales workers (b). Sellers may 'cold call' which can be a nuisance to customers (c).

Now test yourself

TESTED

1 Face-to-face selling involves: [1]
   (a) advertising goods on a website
   (b) a buyer meeting with a seller.
   (c) a seller telephoning buyers to ask them if they want to buy.
   (d) using a website to take orders from customers.
2 John Lewis is one of the UK's most successful retailers. It used to sell all its goods through its department stores in major UK cities, but now it also sells online.
   (a) Identify **two** methods of selling that John Lewis uses. [2]
   (b) Explain **one** advantage to customers of face-to-face shopping at John Lewis. (2)

I can ...

- ☐ Explain how face-to-face selling and telesales operate.
- ☐ Explain the advantages and disadvantages of face-to-face selling to businesses and individual customers.
- ☐ Explain the advantages and disadvantages of telesales selling to businesses and individual customers.

Exam tip

When dealing with different ways of selling, you need to describe your suggested method of selling and explain its advantages and disadvantages.

Influence of e-commerce on business activity

REVISED

The influence of **e-commerce** on businesses is summarised in Figure 4.4.

E-commerce: The bringing together of buying and selling electronically.

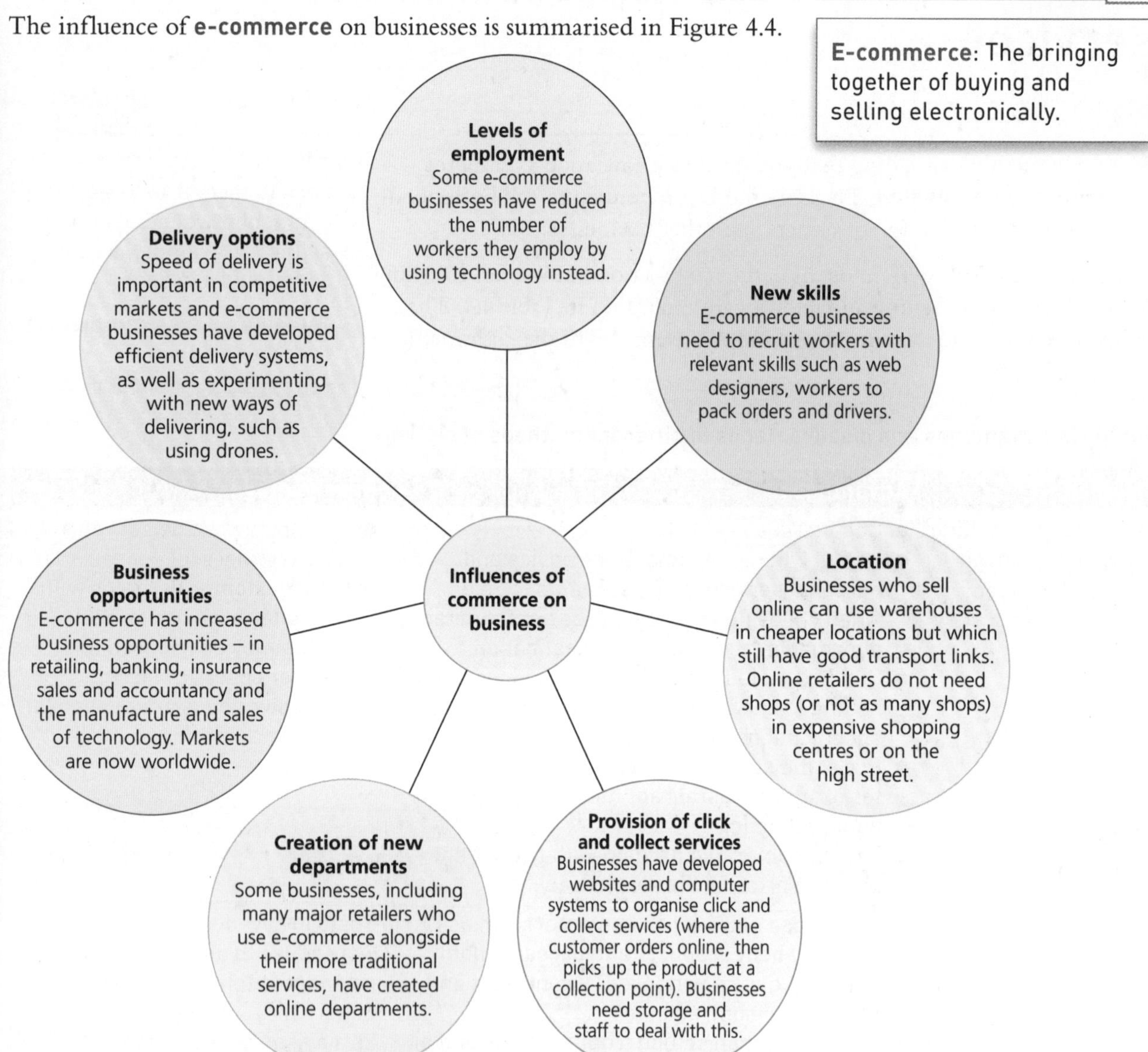

Figure 4.4 Influence of e-commerce on business

The advantages and disadvantages of e-commerce to businesses are summarised in Table 4.5.

Table 4.5 Advantages and disadvantages of e-commerce to businesses

Advantages of e-commerce to businesses	Disadvantages of e-commerce to businesses
Markets have increased as businesses can now sell more easily around the world.	Competition has increased, including greater competition from abroad.
It is possible to sell 24/7.	Delivery systems need to be organised as well as ways of dealing with the increase in goods that are returned.
The costs of selling are usually much lower as a result of savings on rental of premises and a reduction in the number of workers that need to be employed.	E-commerce businesses need to provide cyber security for themselves and their customers.
Web designers can make businesses appear attractive at little cost.	As technology develops so must the e-commerce business, which can add to costs and lead to changes in the operation of the business and the workers it needs.

E-commerce brings some advantages to customers but also some disadvantages. These are summarised in Table 4.6.

Table 4.6 Advantages and disadvantages of e-commerce to customers

Advantages of e-commerce to customers	Disadvantages of e-commerce to customers
Online selling has made it easier for customers to compare prices and find the best deals.	It is impersonal and so customers may not be able to ask questions (unless an online chat option is provided).
Customers can buy 24/7.	Goods are bought as seen and described on the website and they may not be what is wanted when they arrive. Customers must return the goods, often at their own cost.
Choice has increased because customers can buy from sellers around the world.	If the computer systems are not secure, customers may be at risk of personal data theft and bank fraud.
	Not everyone has access to or can use computer technology.

Now test yourself

TESTED ☐

Aldi is a very successful supermarket business. It has grown by selling a limited range of goods at lower prices than its competitors. Although some of Aldi's products are of lower quality, much of its produce is high quality. It does not currently have an e-commerce part of its business that customers could use to order goods online.

1 Explain **two** ways in which Aldi would have to develop its business to make selling via e-commerce possible. [4]
2 Explain **one** benefit customers would gain if Aldi introduced online selling. [2]
3 Explain **one** possible disadvantage for customers of buying online from Aldi. [2]
4 Evaluate the costs and benefits to Aldi of introducing online selling. [7]

Despite the successful growth of its online business, Waterstones has kept many of its shops open.

5 Analyse **one** reason why Waterstones has kept its shops. [3]

Exam tip

Learn lists such as the advantages and disadvantages of e-commerce for both businesses and for customers. If you can remember a number of advantages and disadvantages, it will help you to write answers to questions which require lengthy, well-developed answers.

I can ...

- ☐ Explain how businesses have been influenced by the development of e-commerce.
- ☐ State and explain the advantages and disadvantages of e-commerce to businesses.
- ☐ State and explain the advantages and disadvantages of e-commerce to customers.
- ☐ Evaluate e-commerce from a business point of view.

Importance to a business of good customer service including after-sales service and Contribution of product knowledge and customer engagement to good customer service

REVISED

One of the most important reasons for good **customer service** is that it helps a business to gain and retain customers. The main areas of customer service, and the advantages and disadvantages of each, are described in Figure 4.5.

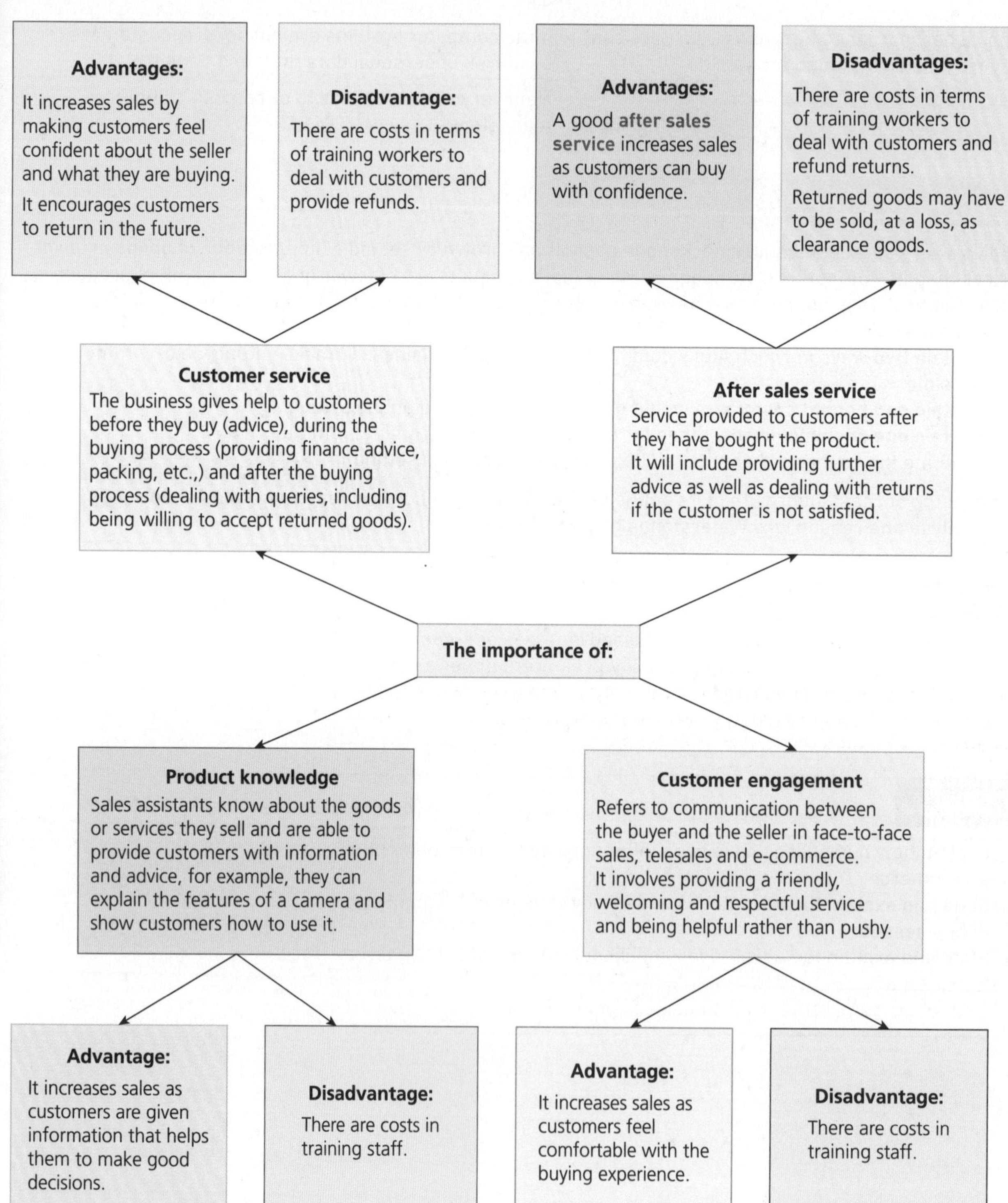

Figure 4.5 Importance of customer service

After-sales service: Advice and help given to a customer after they have bought a product or service.

Customer service: The name given to an area of business that deals with customer enquiries.

Now test yourself

TESTED

Starbucks, the coffee shop chain, had a campaign to improve relationships between their staff and customers. Staff were asked to find out and use the names of customers to make them feel welcome. Customers who gave their first names were given a free drink.

1 The Starbucks campaign to improve relations between staff and customers was designed to improve:
  (a) customer service
  (b) after-sales service
  (c) product knowledge
  (d) customer engagement. [1]

2 Evaluate the benefits of this campaign to Starbucks. [9]

Exam tip

When evaluating, it is useful to think about what evidence you have to make a judgement on whether something had been, or was going to be, successful. This could be information such as sales, revenue, cost or profit data. Weigh these up – for example, is the revenue from extra sales greater than the costs?

I can ...

- ☐ Describe customer service and explain its advantages and disadvantages.
- ☐ Describe after-sales service and explain its advantages and disadvantages.
- ☐ Describe product knowledge and explain its advantages and disadvantages.
- ☐ Describe customer engagement and explain its advantages and disadvantages.

4.4 Consumer law

Impact of consumer law on businesses

REVISED

Although you do not need to be an expert on **consumer law** for the examination, you will find it helpful to know how the law affects businesses and what they sell:

- **Consumer laws** are designed to protect consumers from unscrupulous sellers.
- Laws often apply to both goods and services.
- The key law is the Consumer Rights Act of 2015 which states that goods and services must be 'of **satisfactory quality**,' '**fit for purpose**' and '**as described**'.
- Advertising is controlled by law – it must be legal, decent, honest and truthful.
- Consumers have the right to return faulty goods within 30 days.
- When services are not completed on time, or to a reasonable standard, the consumer can ask for work to be done again, or given a price reduction.

The impact of consumer law on business is summarised in Figure 4.6.

As described: Means that goods must be as the business has described them.

Consumer law: The area of law which protects the customers of a business, mainly through the Consumer Rights Act of 2015.

Fit for purpose: Means that a good or service must do what it is meant to do.

Satisfactory quality of goods: Means that goods should reflect the price charged for them, for example a high-priced product must be of a high quality.

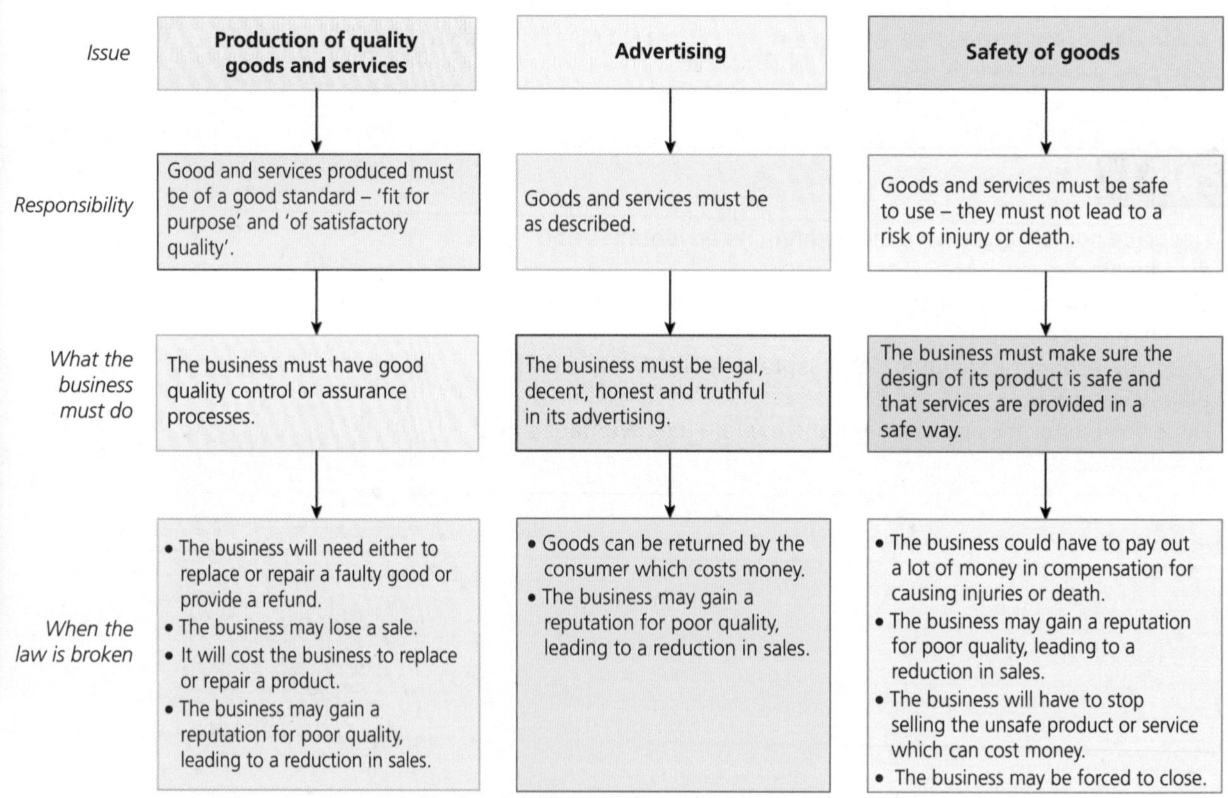

Figure 4.6 Consumer law and its impact on business

Responsible businesses weigh up (evaluate) the risks involved in not acting within the law:

- The examples of 'What the business must do' in Figure 4.6 often mean increased costs for a business.
- When a law is broken, there will be costs for the business, including the loss of **business reputation**.
- Responsible businesses know that it makes financial sense to spend money to ensure they do not break consumer laws as this will save them money and help the business to survive.

Business reputation: Refers to what customers say and feel about a business. Damage to reputation can seriously affect a business.

Now test yourself

TESTED ☐

In 2015, there was an accident involving the 'Smiler' ride at the amusement park, Alton Towers, which resulted in a 17-year-old girl suffering life-changing injuries.

Evaluate the benefits to a business such as Alton Towers of making sure that they provide safe services. [9]

Exam tip

Although you do not need a detailed knowledge of consumer law for the examination, you do need to be able to write about how consumer laws affect the behaviour of businesses and the consequences to business of failing to obey these laws.

I can ...

- ☐ Analyse the effect of consumer law on businesses.
- ☐ Evaluate the benefit to a business of obeying consumer laws.

4.5 Business location

Factors influencing business location

REVISED

Table 4.7 explains the main influences on the **location** of a business and gives an example of each. Although the specification does not show government as an influence, it is an influence on cost, which is why it is included in this table.

Location: Refers to the place where a business is sited.

Proximity: Means 'nearness to.'

Table 4.7 Factors influencing business location

Factor influencing location	Explanation and example
Costs	• Locating in an area where the cost of land, premises or labour is low, such as areas in the north east of the UK, will enable a business to save on the cost of renting an office or factory and on wages. • Businesses need to transport raw materials in and finished goods out, so areas with good road, rail, sea or air links, such as the junction of the M6 and M5 motorways, will keep transport costs low. • Access to reliable and cheap ICT communication, such as fast broadband. London has good ICT facilities but many remote, rural areas do not.
Proximity to the market	• Service businesses must locate near their customers, e.g. a hairdresser will locate near to where consumers live; a department store will be located in a shopping centre where there are lots of customers. • Manufacturing businesses may locate near their customers for easier communication, e.g. a business that makes car components may locate near to the company that purchases them, to enable them to respond quickly to purchase orders. • A business located near its customers may be able to reduce the cost of transporting products to this market, e.g. a local bakery will not transport bread to shops outside its area.
Proximity to labour	• A business needs a supply of skilled workers. 'Silicon Fen' is an area near Cambridge where many ITC firms and skilled workers are located, so an ICT business might wish to locate here. • A business that needs a lot of unskilled labour might locate in an area of high population and/or high unemployment, e.g. Middlesbrough where steel mills have closed, resulting in workers becoming unemployed.
Proximity to materials	• A business may locate near to a source of raw materials to save on transportation costs (particularly when the materials are bulky or heavy), e.g. fish processing businesses are usually located near a fishing port to reduce the need to transport the fish. • Shorter transport journeys are good for the environment as this minimises carbon emissions and enables the business to be more environmentally friendly. A cheese manufacturer may locate near to dairy farms so milk does not need to be transported a long distance.
Government	• The government may give business grants towards start-up costs, or it may reduce corporation tax for those businesses locating to an area of high unemployment, which may encourage firms to locate in enterprise zones, such as in South Wales.

Now test yourself

TESTED

Analyse **one** reason for the location of each of the following. [15]

1. A dentist in the city of Oxford.
2. A pea processing factory in an area of farmland.
3. Asda warehouse near the junction of several motorways.
4. A specialist bank in the financial district of London.
5. A small manufacturing business in an enterprise zone in south Yorkshire.

I can ...

- ☐ List the main factors influencing the location of a business.
- ☐ Analyse and give examples of the main factors influencing the location of a business.

Exam tip

Note that a business' location may be influenced by more than one factor.

4.6 Working with suppliers

Role of procurement

REVISED

The flow chart in Figure 4.7 shows the four stages of **procurement** and explains the decisions made at each stage.

Procurement: The management of purchasing within a business.

Stage of procurement	Influences on decisions	Examples
Identifying goods and services to buy	• Which season the business is buying for. • Changes in technology affect the products a business sells. • Changes in fashion and lifestyle affect the products a business sells.	• A clothes retailer needs to decide what clothes it will sell during the summer months. • A TV retailer will need to decide how many new types of TV to stock and how many old ones. • A food store needs to decide if it should sell more vegetarian meals.
Choosing suppliers	• Dependent on the quality of goods or services consumers want. • Reputation and reliability of suppliers is important.	• A furniture store will need high quality stock. • Next will want to obtain clothing from ethical suppliers (e.g. those that do not use child labour).
Ordering goods and services	• A business completes an order form stating what it wants and sends it to the supplier.	• A bakery will need to send an order for flour to the supplier.
Receiving deliveries from suppliers	• A business will arrange for workers to receive the goods and have an area where they can be stored.	• The owner of a small shop may put goods on shelves as they arrive if they do not have much storage space.

Figure 4.7 Stages in the procurement process

Now test yourself

TESTED

A garden centre sells a range of Christmas decorations in the two months before Christmas.

1 Explain what is meant by the term 'procurement'. [2]

2 Explain the four stages involved in the procurement of Christmas decorations by the garden centre. [8]

Exam tip

An examination question might ask you to write about just one stage in the process of procurement or about the process as a whole.

I can ...

- ☐ Explain what is meant by the term 'procurement'.
- ☐ Explain each of the four stages in the process of procurement.

Impact of logistical and supply decisions on businesses

REVISED

Table 4.8 gives examples of issues that need to be considered and potential problems connected with **logistical** decisions (those involving transportation of goods to customers) and supply decisions (those involving companies the business buys from).

Table 4.8 Logistical issues

Issue	Explanation	Potential problem
Time	The supplier must be able to deliver the goods on time.	The supplier may be short of materials or components and this may delay its production of goods or services. The business could lose sales and revenue as a result.
Reliability	As well as being able to deliver on time, the supplier must be able to supply the quantity and quality of goods needed by the customer.	If the supplier is short of materials or they are not of sufficient quality, it may have to delay or stop production. The business could lose sales and revenue as a result.
Length of the supply chain	A long **supply chain** (one that contains a large number of businesses) has an increased risk of problems occurring along the chain.	A business which makes a component may not get the materials it needs and so cannot produce the components its customer needs to assemble its product.
Costs	The customer will want delivery costs to be as low as possible but this must not be at the expense of reliability.	High delivery costs may make the total production costs too high and the firm may not be able to sell its goods at a profit.
Customer service	A supplier will need to provide a customer service to deal with problems and enquiries from its potential and actual customers.	The business may lose customers if businesses that buy from it are not happy with the service they receive.

Now test yourself

TESTED

In 2016, supermarkets such as Tesco were unable to buy enough custard cream biscuits to meet demand. The biscuits were made by Crawford's Biscuits at its factory in Carlisle. The factory was damaged during winter floods and this led to production being halted while the factory was refurbished. Once production re-started, fuel prices rose in the UK, leading to a rise in the cost of transporting goods.

1. Analyse the impact on Tesco of the problems with the supply chain of custard creams. [3]
2. Analyse how the rise in fuel prices might affect sales of custard creams at Tesco. [3]
3. Analyse the importance of good customer service to firms such as Crawford's Biscuits. [3]
4. Explain:
   (a) what is meant by logistics [1]
   (b) how logistics is involved in the production of custard creams. [2]

Logistics: The process of organising the transport of goods from the seller to the buyer.

Supply chain: The chain of businesses involved in the production of a product and its delivery to the user.

Exam tip

Remember that there may be several businesses in a supply chain, all of which can be affected if there are problems. In the case study example, the businesses that supply Crawford's Biscuits with ingredients and transport firms would also have been affected by what happened.

I can ...

- ☐ Explain the meaning of the terms 'logistics' and 'supply chain'.
- ☐ Analyse how a business can be affected by its supply chain.

5 Finance

5.1 Role of the finance function

Purpose of the finance function *and* Influence of the finance function on business activity

REVISED

The term 'role of the **finance function**' refers to the *jobs* that are done by a **finance** department in a business and these are summarised in Figure 5.1. The work may be done by a department in a large company or by an individual worker in a small business.

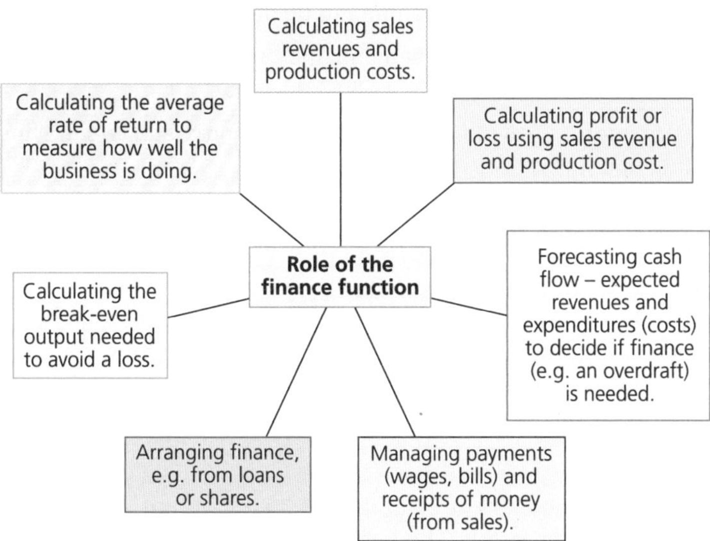

Figure 5.1 **Role of the finance function**

The work of the finance function is important for decision making. For example, a business may want to bring out a new product. The finance function would provide **financial information** about cash flow, spending on marketing, break even, production costs, profits and a comparison of the costs of different types of selling, such as online or through a shop. Other departments will also influence decision making, for example, the production department may suggest the number and types of workers needed and the machinery required. This illustrates how departments in a business are interdependent (see Section 7).

Finance: Money raised and used by a business.

Finance function: This refers to the finance department, which is usually only found in larger businesses. Small business usually employ a firm of accountants to help them with their finance function.

Financial information: Includes details of profit, loss, cash flow, break-even, profit margin and average rate of return. This information is used in business decision-making.

Exam tip

Evaluation involves making a judgement. You may need to say how useful the work of the finance function is to a business. One approach would be to state the ways in which the finance function helps a business to make decisions.

Now test yourself

TESTED

Cheeseman Publishers produces guide books. The finance department has told the business owners that profits are likely to fall. Currently, books are designed in the UK and printed in Italy. The owners have asked the manager to look at ways of reducing costs. They also want to know if it would help if the prices they charge for the books were increased, and if new guide books on different areas would be useful.

Evaluate the importance of the finance department in helping Cheeseman Publishers to be successful. [9]

I can ...

- ☐ Explain the jobs that the finance function does.
- ☐ Evaluate the importance of the finance function.

5.2 Sources of finance

Reasons businesses need finance

REVISED

Some of the reasons businesses need finance are summarised in Table 5.1.

Table 5.1 Why businesses need finance

Need for finance	Explanation
Establishing (setting up) a new business	When a business starts up, it will need to buy items before it can produce or sell anything. For example, it may need to buy or rent a factory, office or shop as well as furniture and machinery.
Funding expansion	If a business decides to increase its scale by producing and selling more goods, it may need to pay for a larger factory, shop or office, along with the furniture and machinery for these. It may need to buy more materials or stocks.
Recruitment	A business will need to recruit workers when it starts up, when it expands and when workers leave and new ones are employed. It costs money to advertise jobs and select workers. Wages and salaries of new staff also need to be paid.
Marketing	Marketing campaigns need to be funded. Advertising and public relations, for example, cost money.
Running the business	All businesses need finance for day-to-day costs such as buying materials, paying expenses such as heating and paying wages.

Now test yourself

TESTED

1 BP is planning to open 20 new filling stations around the country. It will need to raise £5m in finance to buy the land and build the stations. Which of the following describes BP's need for finance? [1]
(a) It is starting up a new business.
(b) It is expanding its business.
(c) It is recruiting new workers.
(d) It is marketing its product.

2 Lidl is a discount supermarket chain. In 2017, it had 670 stores in the UK. Lidl planned to open 50 to 60 new shops in different towns in each of the next two years. The aim was to make it possible for more customers to be able to shop in Lidl stores. Once built, the stores would need to employ staff, buy stock to sell and advertise the new shops to the public. The supermarket chain needed to raise and spend at least £1.45 billion pounds on this investment by 2019.

Using information in the case study, explain **three** reasons Lidl would have to raise finance between 2017 and 2019. [6]

I can ...

☐ List the main reasons why businesses need finance.
☐ Explain the main reasons why business need finance.

Exam tip

Some questions will only need brief details of why businesses need finance. This unit helps with this. Unit 5.2 will give you more details about the finance needs of businesses to use in longer questions.

Ways of raising finance

REVISED

All business need to raise finance. Table 5.2 summarises the advantages and disadvantages of different sources of finance.

Table 5.2 Advantages and disadvantages of different sources of finance.

Source of finance	Advantages	Disadvantages
Owners' capital – the owners' savings are invested.	● No need to repay. ● No interest to pay. ● Does not affect ownership and control.	● Owner risks savings. ● Owner may not have (enough) savings.
Retained profit – money not distributed to the owners (shareholders) as profit.	● No need to repay. ● No interest to pay.	● Business may not have made profits. ● Owners will not get profit as income.
Sale of assets – goods, etc., owned by the business are sold to raise money.	● No need to repay. ● No interest to pay. ● Good if selling off old equipment or stock.	● May be difficult to sell. ● May take time to sell.
Overdraft – a bank makes available to a business more money than they have in their account.	● Meets short-term cash flow problem. ● Interest is only paid on the amount owed. ● Repayment is only due when the business closes or the overdraft is no longer needed.	● Interest is charged for each day money is owed, which can be expensive.
Trade credit – a business sells goods after agreeing to pay for them at a later date.	● The business can have goods to sell before paying for them, via a credit period (usually 30 days but can be up to 90 days). ● No interest if repaid within agreed time limit. ● Can help with a cash flow problem.	● Goods must be paid for even if they do not sell. ● Interest is charged if payment is late.
Taking on a new partner – the new partner invests some of their savings in the business.	● The new partner may bring new skills. ● No need to repay. ● No interest to pay.	● The existing owner(s) will have to give the new partner a say in the running of the business and a share of the profits. ● Partnerships can take on new partners. Sole traders can also do so but must then become partnerships.

Overdraft: An arrangement with a bank that a business can spend more money than it has in its account.

Owners' capital: Money from savings put into the business by the owner(s).

Retained profit: Profit that is not distributed to shareholders as dividend.

Sale of assets: Items sold by the business.

Taking on a partner: Adding a new partner who contributes some new capital.

Trade credit: When the business buys goods to sell and does not need to pay the supplier for a period of time – often 30 days.

Source of finance	Advantages	Disadvantages
Loan – a set amount of money, borrowed for a set period of time.	• Repayment is made in fixed sums over a period of time and usually paid monthly. • The money is available immediately the loan is agreed with the lender (for example, a bank).	• Interest must be paid. • The business may need to give the lender security.
Share issue – new shares are sold to raise more money.	• New investors can contribute a lot of money to the business • No need to repay. • No interest to pay.	• The existing owner(s) will have to give the new shareholders a say in the running of the business and a share of the profits. • Shares can only be sold by limited companies, not by sole traders and partnerships.
Crowdfunding – money is donated or invested by sponsors or people invest to become part-owners of the business.	• New supporters can contribute a lot of money to the business through loans, donations or investing as part-owners. • No need to repay. • No interest to pay.	• Interest will be paid if the money is raised through a loan. • Ownership will be shared if the money is raised through investment.

Crowdfunding: Money raised through an appeal to the public who are supporters of the business.

Loan: A sum of money borrowed for a stated period at an agreed rate of interest.

Share issue: Money raised from investors by selling new shares.

You also need to know which sources of finance are typically used to provide short-term finance and which are used for medium- and long-term finance – see Table 5.3. Note that some sources of finance come under more than one heading, depending on circumstances.

Table 5.3 Short-, medium- and long-term sources of finance

Short-term finance (up to 12 months)	Medium-term finance (1–5 years)	Long-term finance (5 years or more).
Owners' capital	Owners' capital	Owners' capital
Sale of assets	Sale of assets	Sale of assets
Trade credit	Retained profit	Retained profit
	Bank loan	Bank loan
	Crowdfunding	Crowdfunding
		Taking on a new partner
		Share issue

 Now test yourself answers at www.hoddereducation.co.uk/myrevisionnotesdownloads

Now test yourself

TESTED

The main features of different sources of finance and four case studies are shown below.

A No repayment needed.
B Repayment is needed.
C Interest is paid.
D Interest does not have to be paid.
E The number of owners increases, reducing the control of the business of existing owners.
F There are no new owners and existing owners keep control of the business.
G A short-term source of finance.
H A medium-term source of finance.
I A long-term source of finance.

1 Jo Smith runs a small general store selling groceries and other goods. She takes goods on 90-day trade credit from a wholesaler to sell in the shop.
2 Verditek plc is selling new shares to raise the money it needs to produce clean energy. Verditek plc will use the money to expand the business over the next 10 years.
3 Qais Abu Samra is a professional photographer who has a two-year loan of £18,000 from the bank to upgrade his photography studio and equipment.
4 Rajpreet Heir is a wedding organiser. The business has been growing rapidly. She has taken on a new business partner, Alice Curran, to help raise the money needed to open a bigger office. Alice has invested £15,000 of her own savings in the business.

For each case study:

(a) State which of the different sources of finance described above will apply (note there will be more than one source for each situation). [4 × 4]
(b) For each source of finance mentioned, state one advantage and one disadvantage of using it. [4 × 2]

Exam tip

It is very useful to learn the features of different sources of finance. Examination questions may ask you about these features or you can use your knowledge of them to write about why a particular source of finance would be suitable for a given case study (see next section for more on this).

I can ...

- ☐ Explain each source of finance.
- ☐ State whether or not repayment is needed and why.
- ☐ State whether or not interest must be paid.
- ☐ State how the ownership and control of the business is affected by a source of finance.
- ☐ Classify the sources of finance in to short, medium and long term.

How and why different sources of finance are suitable for new and established businesses

REVISED

Businesses need to decide which of the sources of finance available to them they should use. To make this decision, they will evaluate the advantages and disadvantages of **internal finance** and **external finance** by asking a series of questions. Once they have the answers to these questions, they can make their decision. Figure 5.2 gives some examples of the type of questions a business might ask itself.

External finance: Finance raised from sources outside the business. The main external sources of finance are overdraft, trade credit, loan, crowd funding and share issues.

Internal finance: Finance raised from within the business. The main internal sources of finance are owners' capital, retained profit and sale of assets.

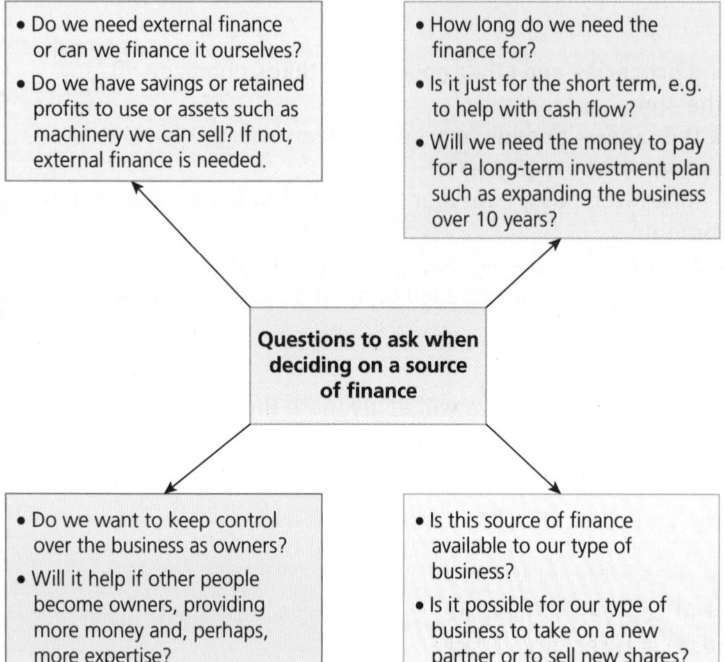

Figure 5.2 Questions to ask when deciding on a source of finance

Now test yourself

TESTED

Gordon Baines runs a business fitting kitchens. He asks customers to pay a 10 per cent deposit towards the cost of the work. He then buys the kitchen units using trade credit. However, Gordon must pay the wages of the workmen who fit the kitchens, often before the customer pays the balance of what they owe. If this happens, Gordon will use either an overdraft facility at the bank or his own savings to pay the wages.

Bowton Airport plc wishes to build a new terminal. The cost of this will be £50m. It is considering a new share issue or a bank loan to raise the money. It does have some retained profit but some shareholders do not want to use this.

Wendy Ingrams plans to open a sunbed salon. She needs £10,000 to buy sunbeds for the salon. She has £4,000 pounds in savings, some of which she will need to use to pay rent on the premises and to pay for some marketing for the business. She is considering asking the bank for a loan.

For each of the above situations, analyse the use of the sources of finance by the businesses concerned. [3 x 4]

Exam tip

Typical questions may ask you to recommend a source of finance to use to finance something or whether a business has used the correct source to finance something. This is an evaluation question. Use the questions in the diagram above to work out an answer. You can also use your knowledge of the features and advantages and disadvantages of sources of finance to work out your answer.

I can ...

☐ Evaluate the use of the different sources of finance.

Now test yourself answers at www.hoddereducation.co.uk/myrevisionnotesdownloads

5.3 Revenue, costs and profits

Concept of revenue in business and its importance in business decision making *and* Calculation of revenue

REVISED

Total **revenue** is the sum of money a business earns from all the sales it makes.

Revenue is important for business because it pays for costs, is a measure of success and, along with costs, determines profits.

Revenue influences business decision making in several ways. For example, if a business wished to increase its revenue, it could opt for one or more of the following:

- Increase the price of the product. This will work if customers do not switch to a cheaper competitor and is likely to succeed if there are few or no competitors.
- Reduce the price to increase sales. This will work if sales rise, perhaps if there are lots of competitors (who do not also reduce their prices).
- Increase its sales by increasing:
  - advertising (targeted correctly and sending the right message)
  - producing more by having a new factory or shop or buying a competitor
  - selling a wider range of products (if customers want to buy these).

However, sometimes a business may not want to make as much as revenue as possible:

- The owner(s) do not want to expand, perhaps to avoid sharing control.
- The business may want to sell to a niche market, for example, selling only to very wealthy people, so they can charge a high price to make their product exclusive.

Revenue: The money received from sales. Q × P = Total revenue where Q is the total quantity sold and P is the price at which the product is sold.

Now test yourself

TESTED

Primark sells clothes at the low-cost end of the market. Several retailers can be considered as competitors in this end of the market including Matalan, New Look, ASDA, H&M and Tesco. There are plenty of more expensive clothes retailers, such as Marks and Spencer, Debenhams and so on.

1 Explain the meaning of the term 'revenue'. [1]
2 Calculate the revenue Primark would make from selling 10,000 t-shirts at £4 each. [1]
3 State **one** reason why revenue is important to Primark. [1]
4 Primark is considering raising its prices to increase its revenue. Evaluate whether this would be successful. [7]

I can ...

- ☐ Define the term 'revenue'.
- ☐ Explain the importance of revenue to a business.
- ☐ List and explain how a business may increase revenue.
- ☐ Analyse and evaluate ways to increase sales.
- ☐ Explain why a business may not wish to make as much revenue as possible.

Exam tip

Be ready for questions that ask you to calculate the amount of revenue a business may earn by learning the formula.

Concept of costs in a business and their importance in business decision making *and* Calculation of costs

REVISED

Example calculations for **variable costs** and **total costs** are shown below.

Example

Total variable costs:

Number of workers × Wage paid to each worker

10 workers × £400 = £4,000

Cost of materials per product × Number of products sold

£3 per product × 6,000 products sold = £18,000

Total variable cost = £4,000 + £18,000 = £22,000

Total cost:

Total **fixed cost** (£12,000) + Total variable cost (£22,000) = £34,000 (total cost).

Fixed costs: Costs that stay the same regardless of a change in output, for example, rent for offices, shops, factories or land and the uniform business tax which is a tax based on the location of the business.

Total costs: The addition of total fixed and total variable costs.

Variable costs: Costs that change as output changes, for example, wage and material costs will increase if more products are made or sold.

Costs are necessary for production to take place and, along with revenue, they determine how much profit a business will make.

A business may want to minimise its costs to help it to:

- increase profits
- reduce prices to become more competitive without cutting profits
- save money in order to expand or to update machinery.

Costs may be reduced by:

- employing new technology instead of workers (although there may be costs in making workers redundant)
- finding cheaper supplies of materials or goods to sell (although the business would need to ensure quality and reliability)
- asking a supplier to reduce its prices or asking workers to take a pay cut. Although suppliers and workers will not want to do this, they may have no alternative but to agree if they could lose sales or their jobs.

Sometimes a business may not need to minimise its costs because, for example, it makes a high-quality product and it knows that its customers are prepared to pay a high price or it does not have any competitors.

Now test yourself

TESTED

Desmond Mills runs a business making pallets which are used by other businesses to transport loads on and off lorries and to move the loads to where they will be stored. Desmond pays £30,000 per year to rent a small factory where the pallets are made and stored. The materials used in the production of pallets are wood and nails which together cost 80p per pallet. One worker can make 20 pallets in an hour. Workers are paid £10 per hour. Pallet making is a very competitive industry. Desmond makes 90,000 pallets per year.

1 State **one** fixed cost and **one** variable cost that Desmond pays. [2]

2 Calculate the:
   (a) cost per pallet for labour (hourly wage ÷ number of pallets made each hour) [1]
   (b) the total variable cost of each pallet (labour cost for each pallet + cost of wood and nails per pallet). [1]

3 Explain how Desmond would calculate the total cost of producing 90,000 pallets. [2]

4 Analyse why total costs are important to Desmond. [4]

I can ...

- ☐ Define the terms 'fixed costs', 'variable costs' and 'total costs'.
- ☐ State examples of fixed and variable costs.
- ☐ Explain the importance of costs to a business.
- ☐ List and explain how a business may reduce costs.
- ☐ Analyse and evaluate ways of reducing costs.
- ☐ Explain why a business may not wish to minimise costs.

Exam tip

Be ready for questions that ask you to calculate the costs of a business. Learn how to calculate total variable costs and total costs.

Concept of profit and loss in business and its importance in business decision making *and* Calculation of profit and loss

REVISED ☐

The concept of profit, at its simplest, is that when the total revenue of a business is more than its total costs of production the business has made a profit.

Example

Total revenue of the business: £22m in revenue

Total costs: £12m

Profit: £10m

A **loss** occurs when the total revenue of a business is less than the total costs of the business.

Example

Total revenue of the business: £56m

Total costs: £80m

Loss: £24m

The examples below show how to calculate the **gross profit** and the **net profit** of a business.

Example

Gross profit is calculated by:

Sales (total revenue) – Cost of sales = Gross profit

Note: the **cost of sales** is the cost of buying in the goods the business sells, or the cost of producing goods.

Sales (total revenue): £35,000

Cost of sales: £15,000

£35,000 – £15,000 = £20,000

Gross profit = £20,000

Example

Net profit is calculated by:

Gross profit – Expenses = Net profit

Note: **expenses** are the costs of running the business.

Gross profit: £20,000

Expenses: £12,000

£20,000 – £12,000 = £8,000

Net profit = £8,000

Cost of sales: The cost to the business of producing goods to sell, for example, buying stock to sell or buying materials and employing workers to make a product.

Expenses: The costs of operating the business, including wages and salaries, rent, or mortgage payments, insurance, heating and lighting and advertising.

Gross profit: Sales minus the cost of sales. In this equation, 'sales' refers to sales income. Sales income is the same as total revenue.

Loss: When the costs of a business are greater than the revenue it makes.

Net profit: Gross profit minus the expenses of operating the business.

Now test yourself

TESTED

BW Trains Ltd makes toy steam trains. The following information is taken from the business accounts of the company:

Total revenue: £8m Cost of sales: £5m

Total costs: £6m Expenses: £1m

Calculate the company's:

1 profit or loss [1]
2 gross profit [2]
3 net profit [2]

I can ...

- ☐ Explain the meaning of the terms 'profit', 'loss', 'gross profit', 'net profit', 'cost of sales' and 'cost of expenses'.
- ☐ Calculate profit and loss.
- ☐ Calculate gross and net profit.

Exam tip

Make sure you learn the formulas and remember to write out the formulas as part of your exam answer – this is a good way to check you are doing the correct calculation.

Calculation and interpretation of profitability ratios

REVISED

The **gross profit margin** is about comparing the total revenue earned by the business with the cost of the sales it makes.

The **net profit margin** is about comparing the gross profit the business earns with its expenses.

Although profit and loss figures are useful, gross and net profit margins give a better indication of how well a business is performing. They can help the business to know where its performance can be improved and whether action needs to be taken. Gross and net profit margins are discussed in Tables 5.4 and 5.5.

Table 5.4 Evaluating improving performance using gross and net profit margins

Performance	Gross profit margin	Net profit margin
Improving performance	Gross profit margin rises, for example: 2018 = 57.1% 2017 = 44%	Net profit margin rises, for example: 2018 = 22.8% 2017 = 18%
Reasons for improvement	● Total revenue rose faster than cost of sales. ● Total revenue fell but cost of sales fell more. ● Total revenue rose and cost of sales fell.	● Gross profit rose faster than expenses. ● Gross profit has fallen but expenses fell more. ● Gross profit rose and expenses fell.

Gross profit margin: Gross profit divided by sales (or total revenue) multiplied by 100.

Net profit margin: Net profit divided by sales (or total revenue) multiplied by 100.

Example

Gross profit margin is calculated by:

$$\frac{\text{Gross profit} \times 100}{\text{Total revenue}} = \text{Gross profit margin}$$

$$\frac{£20{,}000 \times 100}{£35{,}000} = 57.1\%$$

Example

Net profit is calculated by:

$$\frac{\text{Net profit} \times 100}{\text{Total revenue}} = \text{Net profit margin}$$

$$\frac{£8{,}000 \times 100}{£35{,}000} = 22.8\%$$

Table 5.5 Evaluating worsening performance using gross and net profit margins

Performance	Gross profit margin	Net profit margin
Worsening performance	Gross profit margin falls, for example: 2018 = 57.1% 2017 = 64%	Net profit margin falls, for example: 2018 = 22.8% 2017 = 14%
Reasons for worsening performance	• A fall in total revenue and a rise in the cost of sales. • A rise in total revenue but a bigger rise in cost of sales. • A fall in total revenue but a smaller fall in cost of sales.	• A fall in gross profit and a rise in expenses. • A rise in gross profit but a bigger rise in expenses. • A fall in gross profit but a smaller fall in expenses.
Possible Actions	• Increase total revenue by better marketing, for example: – raise (or reduce price) – increase advertising – sell in new markets (e.g. export overseas) – increase the range of products sold. • Reduce cost of sales by, for example: – negotiate a lower price from suppliers – buy from cheaper suppliers.	• Increase total revenue by better marketing – see strategies in column 1. • Reduce expenses by, for example: – reducing the wage bill (reducing hours, cutting hourly pay, replacing labour with machines) – saving on heating and lighting bills.

It is also worth remembering that a business may compare its gross and net profit margins against other similar business to decide if it is performing well enough and if any action is needed.

Exam tip

More formulas here – learn them and remember to write them out in the examination to help you to do the calculation correctly. Be ready to write about why business performance is not good enough and suggest how it can be improved.

Now test yourself

TESTED

1 Food4U is a restaurant selling Chinese takeaway food. The figures below are taken from its accounts:

	Year 1	Year 2
Total revenue	£240,000	£250,000
Gross profit	£76,800	£85,000
Net profit	£36,000	£30,000

(a) Calculate the gross profit margin in Year 1 and Year 2. [2]
(b) Calculate the net profit margin in Year 1 and Year 2. [2]
(c) Evaluate the performance of Food4U in Year 2 compared with Year 1. [3]

2 North West Trains Ltd runs rail services in the north west of the UK. The following information is taken from the business accounts of the company.

	2017	2018
Gross profit margin	37.5%	30%
Net profit margin	25%	20%

(a) Analyse the performance of North West Trains Ltd in 2018 compared to 2017. [2]
(b) Evaluate strategies that North West Trains Ltd could use to improve performance in the future. [9]

I can ...

- ☐ Calculate gross and net profit margins.
- ☐ Use gross and net profit margin figures to evaluate business performance.
- ☐ Analyse and evaluate actions businesses can take to improve performance.

Calculation and interpretation of average rate of return (ARR)

REVISED

Average rate of return (ARR) is used to judge whether investment in the business by its owners is worthwhile – will it give a good enough return? ARR is a forecast – it is based on the *expected* profit the investment will make, compared with the cost of the investment. There are three stages in the calculation of ARR which are shown in Table 5.6. The example uses an investment by a business in a piece of machinery costing £300,000, used over a period of three years – this is the life of the investment.

Average rate of return (ARR): A method of measuring and comparing the profitability of an investment over the life time of the investment.

Table 5.6 Calculating average rate of return

Calculation	Formula	Example
1 Calculate the total profit from the investment over the life of the investment (three years in this example).	Total revenue (from the investment) – Cost of the investment = Profit over the life of the investment	£570,000 – £300,000 = £270,000
2 Calculate the annual average profit per year	$\frac{\text{Total profit}}{\text{Life of the investment (years)}}$ = Average annual profit	$\frac{£270,000}{3}$ = £90,000
3 Calculate the ARR	$\frac{\text{Annual average profit}}{\text{Cost of investment}} \times 100$ = Annual rate of return	$\frac{£90,000}{£300,000} \times 100 = 30\%$

Businesses use ARR to:

- compare different investments, e.g. machine A costs £300,000 and gives an ARR of 30 per cent, while machine B costs £400,000 and produces an ARR of 42 per cent. If the business can afford the extra cost of machine B, this is a better investment because it gives a better average rate of return
- compare an investment with saving, e.g. a business could save £300,000 in a savings account and receive 5 per cent interest or it could invest its £300,000 and receive an ARR of 30 per cent. The ARR shows that it would be better to invest, but if the ARR of the investment was only 3 per cent, it would be better to put the money into a savings account.

Exam tip

Make sure you know how to do the various formulas required to calculate average rate of return. Remember to write them out in the examination to help you when doing a calculation. Questions are also likely to evaluate investment opportunities and will ask you to judge if an investment is worth doing.

Now test yourself

TESTED

Farmer Bill's Adventure Farm offers attractions and activities for families. Farmer Bill's has £200,000 of retained profit in the bank which earns 5 per cent interest. The manager of Farmer Bill's is considering investing in a reptile house to show snakes and lizards to visitors. It will cost £200,000. He has estimated that over a period of 10 years, the reptile house will add £500,000 to the profits of the business.

1 Calculate:
   (a) the total profit Farmer Bill's will make from the reptile house over the period of 10 years. [2]
   (b) the annual average profit Farmer Bill's will make from the reptile house over the period of 10 years. [2]
   (c) the annual rate of return Farmer Bill's will make from the reptile house over the period of 10 years [2]
2 Recommend whether Farmer Bill's should invest in the reptile house. Give a reason for your recommendation. [3]

I can ...

- ☐ Define average rate of return (ARR).
- ☐ Calculate ARR.
- ☐ Evaluate whether an investment is worth doing by comparing the ARR of different options.

5.4 Break-even

Concept of break-even *and* Simple calculation of break-even quantity

REVISED

A business will break even when the revenue it earns from sales is equal to the cost of selling that output. The output at which revenue is equal to cost is called the **break-even quantity**. The business is neither making a profit or a loss. The concept can be applied to a business as a whole or to just one product that the business sells.

Break-even quantity: The amount a business must sell to earn enough revenue to just cover its costs so it does not make a profit or a loss.

The break-even output can be calculated in three ways and these are shown below.

Method 1: Calculating break-even from a table of output, revenue and cost figures

Output – cans of deodorant	Total variable costs (£)	Total fixed costs (£)	Total costs (£)	Total revenue (£)
0	0	8,000	8,000	0
2,000	2,000	8,000	10,000	4,000
4,000	4,000	8,000	12,000	8,000
6,000	6,000	8,000	14,000	12,000
8,000	8,000	8,000	**16,000**	**16,000**
10,000	10,000	8,000	18,000	20,000
12,000	12,000	8,000	20,000	24,000
14,000	14,000	8,000	22,000	28,000
16,000	16,000	8,000	24,000	32,000
18,000	18,000	8,000	26,000	36,000
20,000	20,000	8,000	28,000	40,000

The table shows the costs and revenues for a business producing cans of deodorant, which it sells at £2 each. The variable costs are £1 per can and the fixed cost of production is £8,000.

To find the break-even output, look down the total cost and total revenue columns to see at which output the two are equal. In this example, this is at an output of 8,000 cans.

Method 2: Calculating break-even from a graph

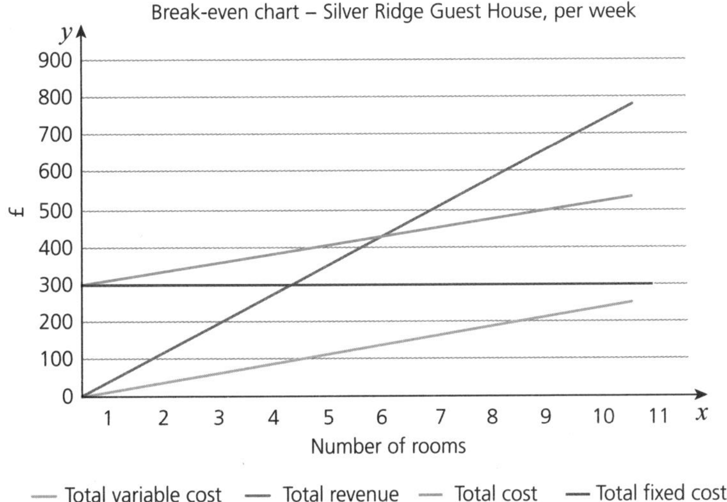

Figure 5.3 Break-even chart for the Silver Ridge Guest House

The graph shows the revenue and costs per week of the Silver Ridge Guest House. The variable cost per room is £25 and the selling price per room is £85. The number of rooms the Silver Ridge Guest House must sell each week to break-even is six. This can be found where the total revenue line crosses the total cost line.

Method 3: Calculating the break-even output using a formula

The formula for calculating break-even and an example calculation are shown below.

$$\text{Break-even output} = \frac{\text{Total fixed cost}}{\text{Contribution per unit}}$$

The contribution per unit is calculated by price minus variable cost per unit.

So the formula can also be written:

$$\text{Break-even output} = \frac{\text{Total fixed cost}}{\text{Price} - \text{variable costs per unit}}$$

Example

A business makes and sells earphones. It sells each set of earphones for £20 (price). The variable cost is £8. The fixed cost is £30,000. The calculation of break-even is shown below.

$$\frac{£30{,}000}{£12} = 2{,}500$$

The business must sell 2,500 sets of earphones to break-even.

Now test yourself

TESTED

Tunstall Pottery makes commemoration pottery objects. Its managing director, Katie Tunstall, is planning to produce a set of figures to commemorate members of the Royal Family. Each figure will cost £60. The variable cost per figure is estimated to be £25. The fixed cost of the Royal Family range will be £700,000.

1 Explain what is meant by the term 'break-even output'. [2]
2 Calculate the number of figures in the Royal Family range that Tunstall Pottery must sell to break-even. [3]

Exam tip

The quickest way to calculate the break-even output from a set of figures is to use the formula. Learn the formula and write it out before putting in the figures so that you know you are performing the correct calculation.

I can ...

- ☐ Explain the term 'break-even quantity'.
- ☐ Calculate the break-even quantity.

Usefulness of break-even analysis in business decision making

REVISED

Break-even forecasts can be used by businesses to plan how much to produce or how much to charge, as described in Figure 5.4.

There are problems with break-even forecasting so businesses need to take care when making decisions based on them. The problems include:

- It is only a **forecast**, a prediction, so things may change in the future.
- The business may not be able to sell at the price planned. New competition in the market may force the price down or demand may be lower at that price, perhaps because incomes have fallen or the price is simply too high.
- Higher than forecast costs may occur if prices of materials or stocks rise.

Break-even forecast: A prediction about the break-even quantity, based on estimates of future sales revenues and costs.

Forecast: A prediction. The forecast break-even output of a business is a prediction.

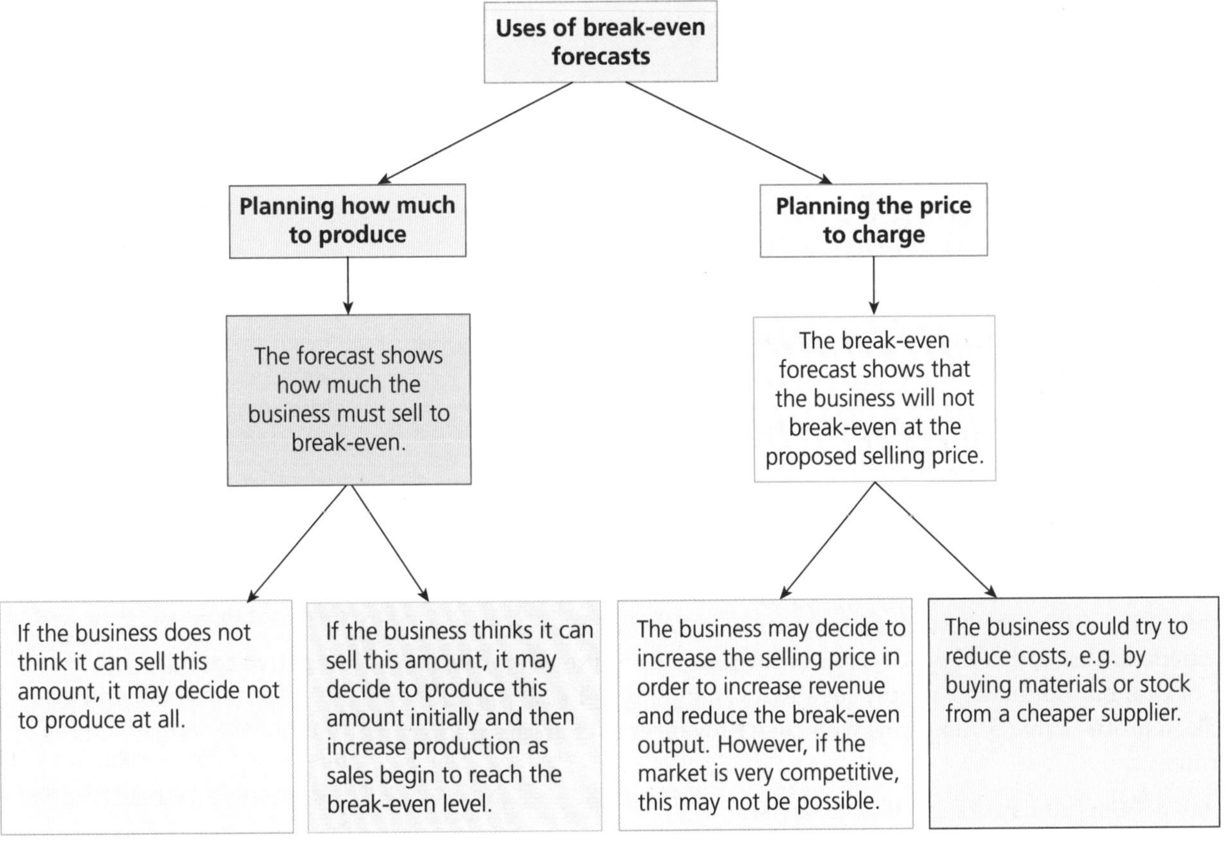

Figure 5.4 Uses of break-even forecasts

Now test yourself

TESTED

Which statement about break-even forecasts is false? [1]

(a) A break-even forecast is a prediction.
(b) By completing a break-even forecast a business will know how much it will sell.
(c) A break-even forecast can help a business decide if it should reduce its costs.
(d) A break-even forecast can help a business decide if it should reduce the price it charges for a product.

Exam tip

Be ready to explain why a break-even forecast may not turn out to be accurate. Make sure your answer goes beyond saying it is only a forecast and explain what changes can affect the forecast.

I can ...

- ☐ Explain the uses of break-even forecasts.
- ☐ Apply the limitations of break-even forecasts to a business.

5.5 Cash and cash flow

Importance of cash to a business *and* Difference between cash and profit *and* Usefulness of cash flow forecasting to a business

REVISED

Cash is money that a business has on its premises or in its bank accounts. Figure 5.5 explains the importance of cash to a business.

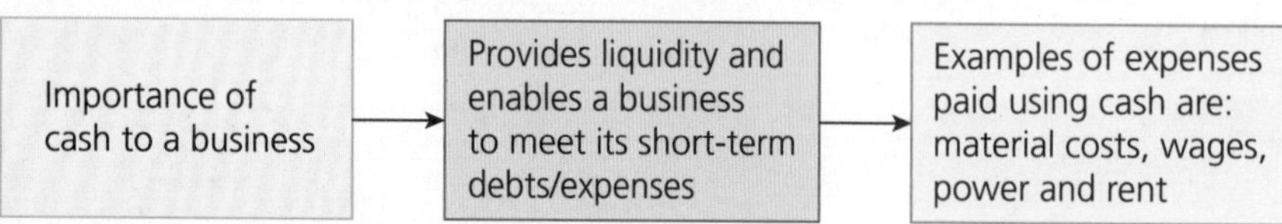

Figure 5.5 Importance of cash to a business

Profit is the difference between sales revenue and production costs. Remember that cash and profits are not the same. A business can have a lot of cash but not make a profit, equally it can be short of cash but still make a profit. Table 5.7 explains why **cash flow forecasts** are useful to a business.

Cash flow forecast: A statement showing the expected flow of money into and out of a business over a period of time.

Liquidity: The ability of a business to pay its short-term debts.

Negative cash flow: A forecast that there will be more cash going out of the business than coming in.

Table 5.7 Usefulness of cash flow forecasts

Use	Explanation
Planning tool	• A cash flow forecast is a plan which will help a business know if it will have **liquidity**. Liquidity is when a business can pay its bills. • A bank manager who sees a well-thought out cash flow forecast is more likely to give a business a loan, especially if there is a **positive cash flow**.
Anticipating periods of cash shortages	• A cash flow forecast might show that the business will have a cash shortage at some time – it does not have liquidity. Knowing this, the business will be able to plan how to deal with this.
Dealing with a cash flow shortage when the business has a **negative cash flow** (it does not have liquidity)	• A shortage can be dealt with by: – arranging for finance (usually an overdraft, though this will mean paying interest) so the business can pay its bills (e.g. wages, suppliers) to continue production – trying to reduce spending or increase revenue to avoid the shortage.
Providing targets	• A business may set a target for cash held so it knows it can pay bills during a period of negative cash flow.

Note: Cash flow forecasts are not always accurate. Sales may not be as high as expected, the price lower and the costs higher. Sales may be affected by the weather or changes in the economy (for example, changes to people's employment and incomes). Costs may rise or fall depending on economic conditions.

Positive cash flow: A forecast that there will be more cash coming into the business than going out.

Now test yourself

TESTED

Which of these statements about cash flow is correct? [1]

(a) A business that has a negative cash flow cannot make a profit.
(b) A negative cash flow is a sign that the business is badly managed.
(c) A negative cash flow may be financed using an overdraft.
(d) A business that has a negative cash flow will not get a loan from a bank.

I can ...

- ☐ Explain the importance of cash to a business.
- ☐ Explain the difference between cash held by a business and the profits of a business.
- ☐ Explain the usefulness of cash flow forecasts
- ☐ Evaluate ways of dealing with cash flow problems.

Completion of cash flow forecasts

REVISED

Table 5.8 shows the cash flow forecast for a convenience shop in Bowton. Its cash inflow comes from selling groceries and newspapers and renting out two apartments above the shop. Its cash outflow is payments for stock, heating and lighting bills, workers' wages and interest and loan repayments due each month.

Table 5.8 Cash flow forecast – convenience shop, Bowton

Cash flow forecast – convenience shop				
	January	**February**	**March**	**April**
	£	**£**	**£**	**£**
Cash inflow				
Sales	100,000	80,000	60,000	70,000
Rental income	10,000	10,000	10,000	10,000
Total inflow	110,000	90,000	70,000	80,000
Cash outflow				
Stock	50,000	80,000	60,000	40,000
Energy costs	5,000	10,000	5,000	5,000
Wages	10,000	30,000	20,000	10,000
Interest and loan repayments	10,000	15,000	10,000	5,000
Total outflow	75,000	135,000	95,000	60,000
Net cash flow	**35,000**	**-45,000**	**-25,000**	**20,000**
Opening balance	25,000	60,000	15,000	-10,000
Closing balance	60,000	15,000	-10,000	10,000

The notes below explain how the cash flow statement is drawn up.

1. Cash that flows in is added up and the total for each month is put in the 'Total inflow' row.
2. Cash that flows out is added up and the total for each month is put in the 'Total outflow' row.
3. Total outflow is deducted from total inflow each month and this is the '**Net cash flow**'. The **opening balance** is the cash the business has at the start of the month (usually kept in its bank account).
4. Net cash outflow is added to the opening balance if it is a positive or deducted from the opening balance if it is a negative. This gives the '**closing balance**' (cash the business has at the end of the month). This becomes the opening balance for the next month.

Cash: Notes and coins held in the business plus money it has in its bank accounts.

Closing balance: The amount of cash left at the end of the month. It becomes the opening balance for the next month.

Net cash flow: Total inflow of cash minus total outflow.

Opening balance: The amount of cash available at the beginning of the month. It is the closing balance for the previous month.

Profit: The total revenue a business receives minus the total costs of production.

Notes:

- For January and April, the shop is forecasting a positive cash flow.
- For February and March, the shop is forecasting a negative cash flow.
- For January, February and April, the shop is forecasting a positive closing balance. The shop has cash at the end of the month.
- For March, the shop is forecasting a negative closing balance. This means the business does not have enough cash to pay all its bills. It could finance this by using an overdraft or it could delay payment of some of its bills to avoid this. Note that a negative cash flow may not be a problem if it is temporary.

Now test yourself

TESTED

The cash flow forecast below is for Bowton Garage Ltd for the first three months of the year.

Cash flow forecast – Bowton Garage Ltd			
	January	**February**	**March**
	£	**£**	**£**
Cash inflow			
Sales	35,000	25,000	30,000
Total inflow	35,000	25,000	30,000
Cash outflow			
Materials	8,000	8,000	6,000
Electricity and gas	1,000	1,000	1,000
Rent paid for premises	2,000	2,000	2,000
Wages	14,000	**A**	14,000
Total outflow	25,000	22,000	23,000
Net cash flow	10,000	3,000	7,000
Opening balance	5,000	15,000	18,000
Closing balance	15,000	18,000	**B**

Now test yourself

TESTED

1. Explain the meaning of the term 'cash flow forecast'. [2]
2. Calculate the missing figures in the cash flow for Bowton Garage Ltd:
   A – the wages paid by Bowton Garage Ltd in February.
   B – the closing balance for March. [2]
3. Explain the meaning of the following terms:
   (a) Total inflow (b) Net cash flow (c) Opening balance [3]
4. State one reason why drawing up a cash flow forecast is useful for Bowton Garage Ltd. [2]
5. If Bowton Garage Ltd had a negative cash flow, explain two ways in which the business could deal with it. [4]

Exam tip

An examination question will often test your understanding of cash flow forecasts by giving you an incomplete example and asking you to fill in the missing spaces. To do this, you need to understand how a cash flow forecast is drawn up. A question may include a negative cash flow forecast as this is a good opportunity to ask candidates to think of a solution to the problem. Always give reasons for any recommendations you make.

I can ...

- ☐ Explain the term 'cash flow forecast'.
- ☐ Explain the terms used in a cash flow forecast.
- ☐ Calculate missing figures in a cash flow forecast.

Now test yourself answers at www.hoddereducation.co.uk/myrevisionnotesdownloads

6 Influences on business

6.1 Ethical and environmental considerations

Ethical considerations in businesses

REVISED

What is **ethical** or right or wrong is not always clear. Some people think that it is unethical to use animals to test products such as cosmetics or medicines, while others think this is acceptable as it stops humans being damaged by unsafe products. Animal rights supporters say that there are other ways of testing without involving animals. Figure 6.1 describes some ethical considerations that a business might consider.

Ethical: Concerned with what is right and wrong or behaving in a morally correct way.

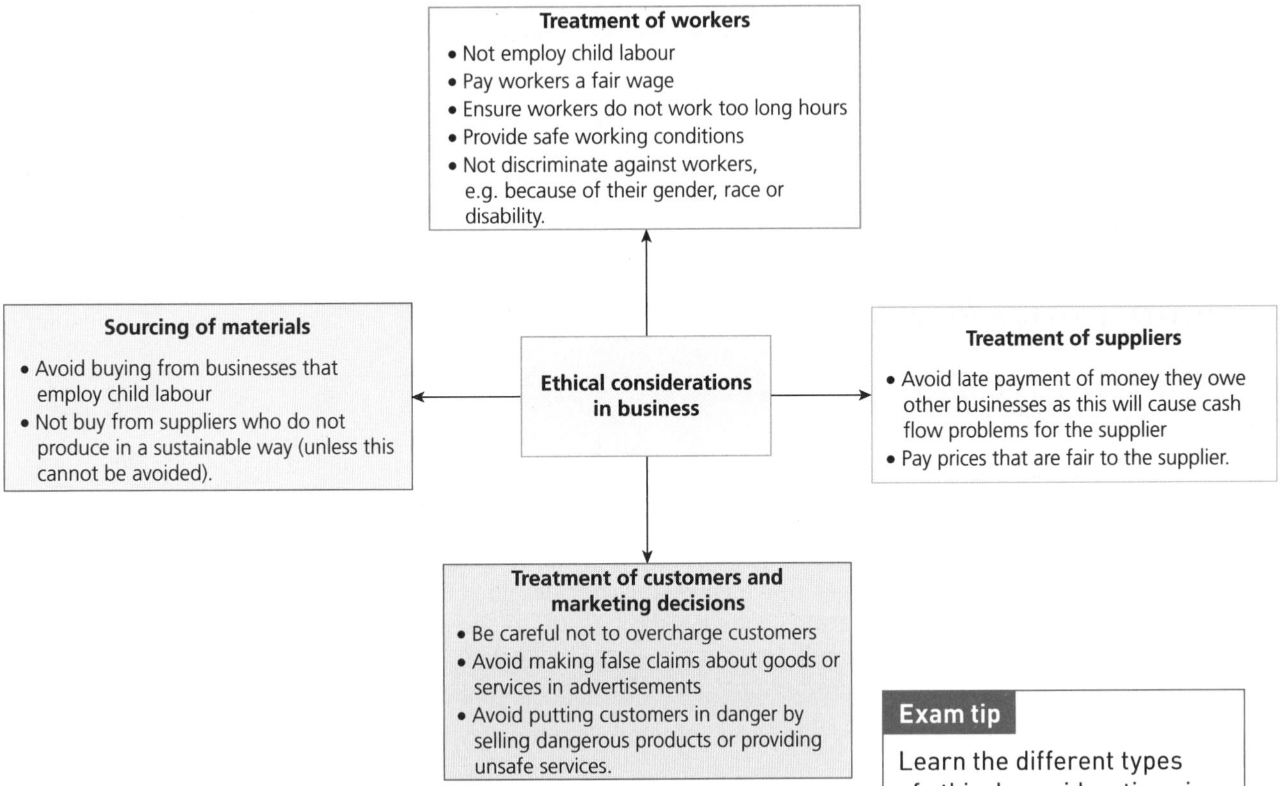

Ethical considerations in business

Treatment of workers
- Not employ child labour
- Pay workers a fair wage
- Ensure workers do not work too long hours
- Provide safe working conditions
- Not discriminate against workers, e.g. because of their gender, race or disability.

Sourcing of materials
- Avoid buying from businesses that employ child labour
- Not buy from suppliers who do not produce in a sustainable way (unless this cannot be avoided).

Treatment of suppliers
- Avoid late payment of money they owe other businesses as this will cause cash flow problems for the supplier
- Pay prices that are fair to the supplier.

Treatment of customers and marketing decisions
- Be careful not to overcharge customers
- Avoid making false claims about goods or services in advertisements
- Avoid putting customers in danger by selling dangerous products or providing unsafe services.

Figure 6.1 Ethical considerations in businesses

Exam tip

Learn the different types of ethical considerations in business and be ready to apply these to a case study.

Now test yourself

TESTED

Some private health firms have been accused by the UK National Screening Committee of doing unnecessary tests on patients. Patients have been charged up to £2,000 for tests such as MRI scans, heart tests and cancer tests. Doctors think that some of the tests may cause problems as they can lead to anxiety, may give a false diagnosis and may even result in treatment that is not needed.

1 State **four** ethical considerations in business. [4]
2 State and explain how the health firms conducting unnecessary health tests may be considered unethical. [3]

I can ...

- ☐ State and explain ethical considerations in business.
- ☐ Analyse how a business practice may be considered ethical or unethical.

Impact of ethical considerations on businesses

REVISED

Table 6.1 shows the possible advantages and disadvantages for a business that behaves ethically. Ethical and unethical behaviour can affect the costs, sales, profits and investments of a business.

The ethical or unethical behaviour of one firm may also impact on another firm. For example, if customers find out that a business that claims to be ethical buys stock from an unethical supplier (whether knowingly or unknowingly), it can affect the business' reputation.

Table 6.1 Advantages and disadvantages of behaving ethically in business

Possible advantages	Possible disadvantages
Costs may be lower because workers who are paid fairly and work in safe conditions are well-motivated so productivity is high. They are less likely to look for jobs elsewhere, increasing retention and reducing training and recruitment costs, and it will be easier and cheaper to recruit additional new workers.	Costs may be higher because the business may have to pay more for fair wages or because it does not employ cheaper child labour. There are also costs involved in health and safety provision and purchasing ethically-produced goods.
Sales may be higher because a reputation for being ethical will lead to trust from customers. Some business buyers only want to buy from ethical suppliers to protect their own reputation.	Sales may be lower because the business is honest with customers in its advertising and does not sell goods to customers they do not need.
Profits may be higher because there may be higher sales and lower costs.	Profit may be lower because the business charges a lower price than its competitors or pays higher costs than its competitors or customers prefer to buy from an unethical producer if its prices are lower.
Investment may be higher because some investors only want to invest in ethical businesses.	Investment may be lower because profits may not be as high, which may put some investors off investing.

Now test yourself

TESTED

Sports Direct sells sports clothing and accessories. In 2015, newspapers reported that Sports Direct was treating its warehouse workers unfairly. The reports indicated that the business was paying workers less that the National Minimum Wage, searched them intrusively when they finished work and used zero-hours contracts (some workers got little, or no work in some weeks). That year, company sales fell and on one day the share price fell by 11 per cent as investors decided to sell their shares. Sports Direct claims it has now improved the way it operates and says pay has increased and all workers are guaranteed a minimum of 12 hours work each week. However, many of those who work in the warehouse at Sports Direct are supplied by agencies, so were unaffected by these changes.

Evaluate the possible effects on Sports Direct of improving the way it treats its workers. [9]

I can ...

- ☐ State and explain ways in which businesses may be affected by ethical or unethical behaviour.
- ☐ Evaluate the impact of ethical considerations on a business.

Exam tip

You may be asked to evaluate the advantages or disadvantages of ethical practices of a business in a case study. If the information is inconclusive, you can write that the answer depends on the effect on costs, sales, profit and investment.

Environmental considerations in businesses

REVISED

Table 6.2 describes the four environmental considerations you need to learn.

Table 6.2 Environmental considerations

Environmental consideration	Explanation	Example
Sustainability	When the production and sale of a product involves the use of renewable resources, rather than scarce resources.	Wind and solar power are examples of renewable resources which generate sustainable electricity. A business that uses this type of energy is **environmentally friendly**. Electricity generated from coal is not sustainable because it uses up coal stocks.
Waste disposal	Waste disposal is environmentally friendly only if a business reduces, reuses or recycles its waste.	A business which recycles the aluminium cans that it uses is environmentally friendly, while a business which sends the cans to land fill is not.
Pollution	Pollution is the introduction of something harmful into the environment as a result of the activity of a business. Pollution can affect air, rivers and people's hearing in the form of noise.	A business that switches from diesel to battery-powered cars is helping to reduce air pollution.
Climate change	Climate change occurs when weather patterns change or average temperatures rise or fall.	A business that burns fossil fuels helps to raise average temperatures, which is an example of global warming. This in turn is leading to changes in the seasons and unusual weather patterns.

Climate change: When average temperatures rise or fall and patterns of weather change.

Environmentally friendly: Describes consumers and businesses that act to make production sustainable.

Pollution: Causing harm to the environment, including air, land and water.

Sustainability: Production that does not lead to the depletion of natural resources.

Waste disposal: The process of getting rid of unwanted materials.

Now test yourself

TESTED

Which statement is false? [1]

(a) An environmentally-friendly business will not produce any waste products at all.
(b) An environmentally-friendly business will recycle waste products where possible.
(c) An environmentally-friendly business will minimise its use of non-renewable resources.
(d) An environmentally-friendly business will minimise the pollution it causes.

I can ...

- ☐ State and explain environmental considerations in business.
- ☐ Explain how businesses may respond to environmental considerations

Exam tip

There is some overlap between the different environmental considerations. Make sure that you explain your points fully and clearly.

Impact of environmental considerations on businesses

REVISED

The impact of an environmental consideration on a business depends on how the business responds to it.

Environmentally friendly production can affect costs, sales, taxes, subsidies, profits and capital costs.

Table 6.3 Advantages and disadvantages of being environmentally friendly for a business

Advantages of being environmentally friendly	Disadvantages of being environmentally friendly
Costs may be lower because a business may have taken steps to use less energy or create less waste, reducing energy bills and waste disposal costs.	Production costs may be higher if materials produced in an environmentally-friendly way are more expensive.
Sales may be higher because customers may prefer to buy from a business that care about the environment.	Sales may be lower if the business charges higher prices to cover any extra costs of environmentally-friendly production.
Lower taxes and avoidance of paying fines may occur because the business creates less pollution.	Capital costs may rise if the business invests in new machines and plant to produce in an environmentally-friendly way.
A business may gain subsidies from the government to help pay for environmentally-friendly production.	
Profits may be higher because sales revenue rise and costs fall.	

Businesses that fail to be environmentally-friendly may lose out on the advantages this can bring and this may make it difficult for them to compete. However, they will also avoid the disadvantages associated with being environmentally friendly and this might give them a competitive advantage.

Whether it is better for a business to be environmentally friendly depends on a number of factors:

- Some business owners view being environmentally-friendly as the 'right' thing to do and want to protect the planet and its people, now and in the future.
- If customers place importance on environmentally-friendly production, this will help sales, but sometimes they just want low-price goods and this may (though not always) favour businesses that do not use environmentally-friendly production.
- Sometimes businesses based in a country with strict environmental regulations struggle to export to countries where businesses that are less environmentally-friendly are allowed to sell.

Exam tip

Remember that with evaluation questions you must give two sides of the argument and then come to a conclusion by weighing them up.

Now test yourself

TESTED

Northumbrian Water is the sole provider of water supplies and sewage disposal services to all households in Northumberland. The Environment Agency reported that Northumbrian Water had been fined £375,000 because it pumped raw sewage into a river. Northumbrian Water has spent money on investment so that this problem does not happen again, as well as paying to clean up the damage it had caused.

Evaluate the impact on Northumbrian Water of allowing raw sewage to be pumped into a river. [9]

I can ...

- ☐ State and explain the impact on businesses of environmental considerations.
- ☐ Evaluate the impact of either failing to deal with environmental considerations or of dealing successfully with them.

6.2 The economic climate

The economic climate and its impact on business

REVISED

The **economic climate** is made up of two main elements:

- **Consumer income** levels: the level of income received by people in a country is important for businesses because it influences how much money people have to spend on goods and services.
- Employment and unemployment levels: employment and unemployment levels influence income. A person in work will earn a wage or salary and will often have more income than a person who is unemployed, who may only receive welfare benefits.

The **level of income** and **level of employment** are linked. When employment rises, the level of income usually rises. When employment falls, unemployment rises and when employment rises, unemployment will usually fall.

These changes in income and employment have an impact on businesses on sales, production and profits as well as on business strategy.

Consumer income: The amount of money consumers receive from work and from assets they own such as shares and property.

Economic climate: Refers to how well the country is doing in terms of levels of income and employment.

Level of income: The average income of people in a country.

Level of unemployment: The number of people out of work in a country.

Impact on sales, production and profits

Figure 6.2 summarises the possible impacts of rising levels of income and employment on business.

Figure 6.2 Possible impacts on businesses of rising income and employment

Note the following as they are useful evaluation points:

- The impact of economic changes on business will depend on what kind of goods it sells.
- The bigger the change in income, the greater the impact on businesses.
- Falling income and employment will have the opposite effects of those described above.

Impact on business strategy

Business strategy is what the business does in response to a change in income and employment. Figure 6.3 shows possible ways in which businesses may change what they do when income and employment fall.

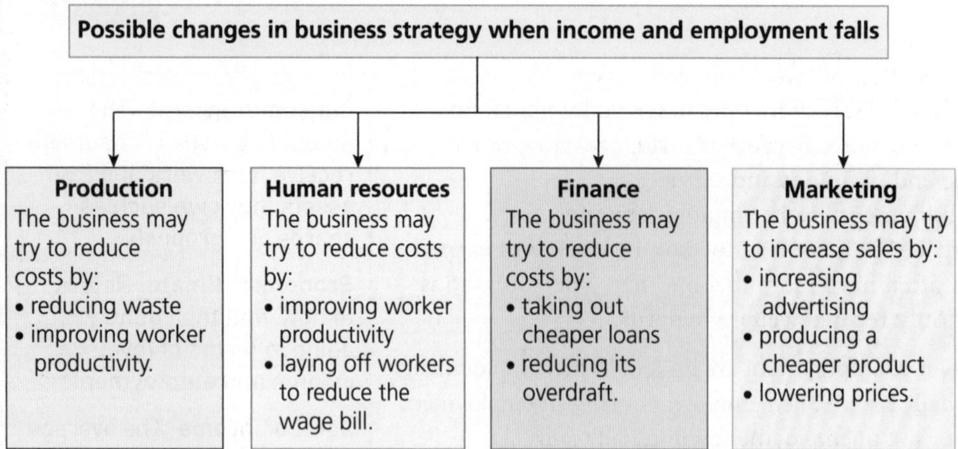

Figure 6.3 Possible changes in business strategy due to a fall in income and employment

Now test yourself

TESTED

1 Which of the following statements is true? [1]
(a) The sales of a business will always increase when incomes rise.
(b) Rising incomes often lead to an increase in the sales of luxury goods.
(c) A rise in unemployment will make all consumers worse off.
(d) A fall in consumer income will always cause a business to sell less.

2 In 2017, Dixons Carphone experienced falling sales of mobile phones. One reason for this, they said, was that the level of real income was falling. As a result, customers were holding onto their mobile phones longer, rather than buying newer models. The company announced that it expected its profits to fall.
In 2009, Poundland reported a big increase in sales. Poundland is a retailer that sells a large variety of goods, including clearance items usually sold at supermarkets or other retailers as well as some 'own brand' goods. Most items are sold at £1 and the goods are often cheaper than in other retail stores. At the time, there was a recession in the UK and the level of real income was falling.
(a) Analyse why, at times of falling real income, Poundland increased its sales while sales at Dixons Carphone fell. [6]
(b) Recommend how Dixons Carphone could have changed its marketing to minimise the fall in sales it was expecting. Give a reason for your recommendation. [3]

I can ...

- ☐ Explain the terms 'level of income' and 'level of employment'.
- ☐ Analyse the impact of changes in income and employment on businesses.
- ☐ Evaluate the factors which influence the impact on a business when income and employment levels change.
- ☐ Recommend strategies that businesses can use when income and employment levels change.

Exam tip

Useful evaluation points include the size of changes in income and employment, how different kinds of businesses will be affected and different ways in which businesses can respond to changes in the economic climate.

6.3 Globalisation

Concept of globalisation

REVISED

Globalisation is the process by which businesses around the world have become increasingly interconnected. Figure 6.4 shows the main ways in which this may happen:

Globalisation: The process by which business activity around the world has become increasingly interconnected.

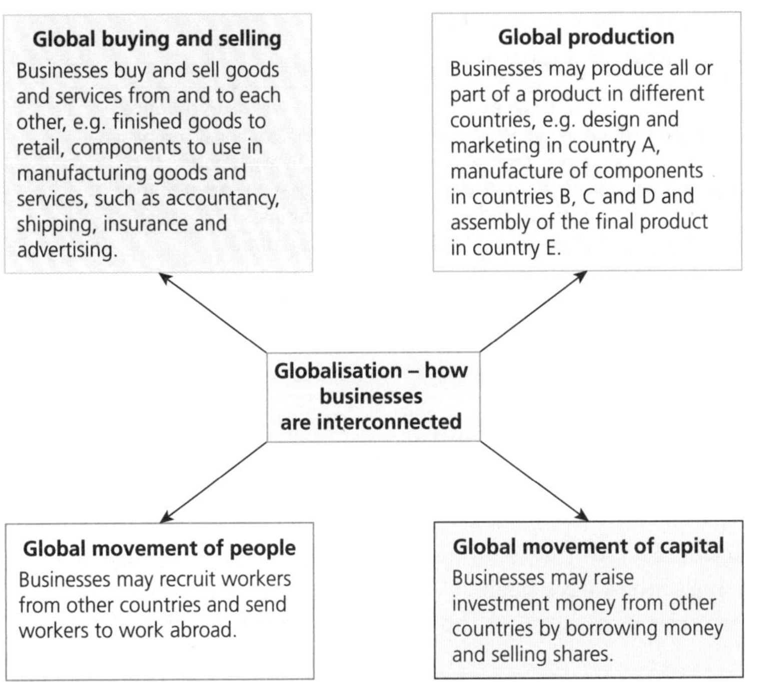

Figure 6.4 Globalisation of businesses

Globalisation has been made easier for the following reasons:

- Improvements to transport: larger ships and planes and better road and rail networks have led to a reduction in transport costs.
- Better telecommunications and the internet: websites, email, social media, telephone and video-conferencing have reduced costs and made it easier to arrange international business or to share plans and knowledge.
- Reduced trading barriers: a reduction in tariffs (taxes on imports) and quotas (limits on the amount that can be imported) as countries agree to trade deals or to free trade arrangements. Tariffs and quotas can make it uncompetitive for businesses to export.

Exam tip

Apply your answers to the business given in the case study as much as possible. The case study is intended to help you understand what the question means, but also tests whether you can apply your knowledge to the business given in the case study.

I can ...

- ☐ State and explain the different ways in which businesses around the world are interconnected.
- ☐ Explain why globalisation has increased.

Now test yourself

TESTED

Jaguar Land Rover (JLR) makes cars and its headquarters is in the UK. The cars are sold in many countries around the world, including the USA and in the Far East. Cars are assembled in the UK and China. Components used in the cars come from many countries, for example, gear boxes are made in the Czech Republic and tyres in Italy. The UK offices and factories employ workers from many countries other than the UK, such as engineers from Romania, Spain, India and Australia. UK workers go to work in China and Germany. Services are bought from the UK and other countries, including India. The business is owned by TATA, an Indian business. Communications between the UK HQ and its business in China have been helped by the development of ICT and UK managers can now easily send designs and talk about quality issues with workers in China. Transport costs have reduced as bigger ships are now used to carry greater numbers of cars. JLR has also favoured countries developing free trade deals.

1 Explain **two** ways in which JLR can be said to be involved in globalised trade. [4]
2 Explain **one** reason why JLR has been able to become a global business. [2]

Impact of globalisation on businesses

REVISED

The impact of globalisation is discussed under four headings. There is some overlap between the sections but this will help with your understanding.

Growth of multinational companies

Multinational companies (MNCs), such as Coca Cola and Google, are examples of globalisation. They operate in more than one country. The advantages to the business of being an MNC are shown in Figure 6.5.

1 Increased sales	2 Risk is spread	3 Lower costs	4 Tax avoidance
Each country has more potential customers.	Sales are not dependent on one country. Sales in one country may be low, but not in all the countries where the business sells.	Production of part or all of a good or service can take place in a country with low costs, for example, one that has cheaper land or labour.	Multinational companies can avoid paying tax by locating part(s) of their business in low tax countries.

Figure 6.5 Advantages of being a multinational company

Influence on business location

Globalisation has influenced where businesses choose to locate. Some businesses have chosen to locate part of their production abroad, perhaps keeping their headquarters in the country where the business started. However, some businesses have moved production back to the UK from abroad because the advantages of producing abroad have been lost over time (for example, wages in other countries have risen) or the disadvantages have proved too great.

International brand: An image or values for a product that are communicated in countries around the world.

Multinational companies: Businesses that operate in different countries around the world.

Advantages of locating abroad

- Lower production costs, for example, because labour, land, property and technology is cheaper in some countries.
- Expert/skilled workers may be in plentiful supply in some countries but not in the country where the business currently produces.
- The business can be located near to the market (its customers).

Disadvantages of locating abroad

- Quality control may be difficult as managers in the headquarters may not be able to check work easily.
- Transport costs may be higher if the goods are not sold where they are produced.
- Sales may be lost if customers do not like goods being made abroad (e.g. they prefer 'made in Britain').
- Skilled labour is not always available.
- Productivity may be low if workers are unskilled, leading to a rise in production costs.

International branding

Businesses that sell in many different countries need to think about how they will market their goods and services in a way that will suit the local market – they need to create an **international brand**. Figure 6.6 shows some considerations they need to think about.

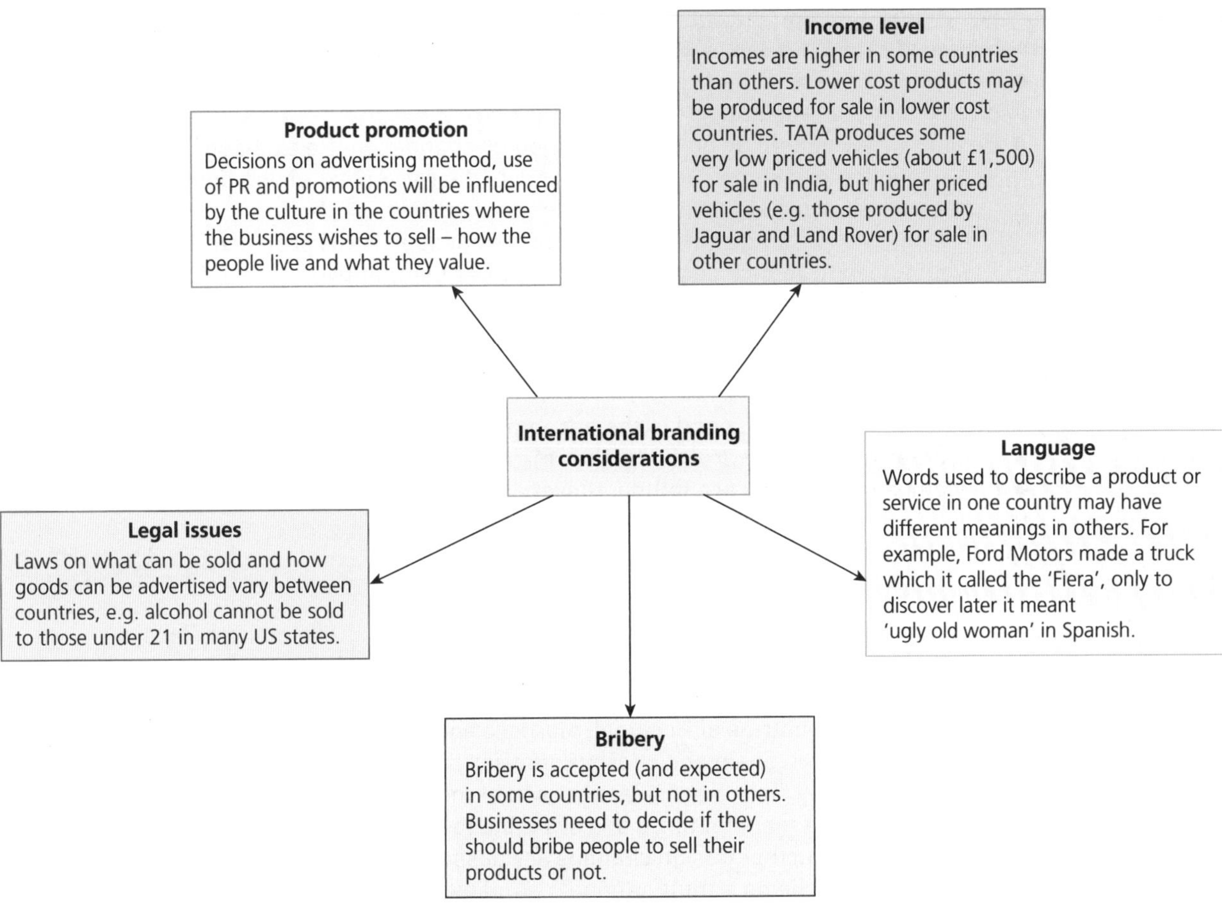

Figure 6.6 International branding considerations

How businesses compete internationally

Businesses that compete internationally sell goods and services abroad and in the UK where overseas firms also compete. Table 6.4 summarises the factors which influence how businesses compete internationally.

Table 6.4 Factors which influence how businesses compete internationally

Factor	Influence
Growth	• Expand overseas, for example, open shops in other countries.
Marketing	• Make products to suit different countries. • Promote goods and services in different countries. • Set prices that are affordable in different countries. • Locate outlets in specific places in different countries where there will be customers.
Human resources	• Recruit, train and motivate local workers. • Establish good communications with workers in different countries so that production is efficient. • Obey laws about employing workers in different countries.
Business operations	• Choose the most efficient method of production for the location, such as changing from batch to flow production to reduce costs or introducing technology. • Ensure good quality assurance processes to guarantee products/services produced in different countries maintain the same standards. • Provide an appropriate sales process (online or face to face) for the country in which it is selling. • Locate locally to be near the market.
Finance	• Arrange loans, overdrafts and sales of shares that may be needed abroad. • Make sure the costs of selling abroad can be covered.

Factor	Influence
Exchange rate	● The exchange rate is the price of one currency in terms of another. It influences the price of exports and imports. ● Business may benefit or be disadvantaged by changes in the exchange rate: – A rise in the exchange rate makes exports dearer. An exporting business would need to reduce costs to keep its prices competitive. – A fall in the exchange rate makes imports cheaper. A UK producer selling in the UK would need to reduce costs to keep its prices competitive.
Ethical and environmental influences	● Businesses that wish to be ethical need to consider the wages, who they employ (avoiding child labour) and health and safety wherever they produce, so that consumers have confidence in them.
Economic climate	● Businesses need to respond to the economic climate in the countries where they sell. ● If incomes in a country are rising, they may be able to sell more. ● If incomes in a country are falling, they may need to reduce prices to maintain sales.

Now test yourself

TESTED ☐

Spanish retailer Zara sells a range of fashion clothing in what is a very competitive market. Zara is a multinational company which sells through around 2,100 shops and online in 88 different countries, including Spain, UK, USA, Canada, China, South Korea, South Africa and India. Zara produces clothes in its Spanish factories, in the nearby countries of Portugal, Morocco and Turkey and in Asia where there are many low-paid workers. Locating in Spain and nearby countries makes communications between its headquarters and its factories easy. This means Zara is good at meeting changing consumer needs, introducing new designs which can be manufactured and available to buy within about four weeks. If these are not quite what consumers want, further design changes are possible within two to three weeks.

1 Explain **one** advantage to Zara of being a multinational company. [2]
2 Analyse **one** advantage to Zara of producing clothes in nearby countries. [3]
3 Analyse why, as a multinational company selling in many different countries, it is important to Zara to be able to change designs quickly. [3]
4 Analyse how a rise in the value of the euro (the currency used in Spain) against the pound would affect the price and sales of clothes made in Spain but which are exported to the UK. [6]

Exam tip

Two useful evaluation strategies include:

- discuss the extent of changes, for example, how much the exchange rate changes will decide how much import and export prices rise or fall
- weigh up advantages and disadvantages that apply to the business as it stands.

I can ...

- ☐ Analyse and evaluate the advantages to a business of being a multinational company.
- ☐ Analyse and evaluate the advantages and disadvantages of locating abroad (or in the UK for an overseas business).
- ☐ Analyse and evaluate the main considerations that affect a business when creating an international brand.
- ☐ Analyse and evaluate the different ways in which businesses compete internationally.

7 The interdependent nature of business

The interdependent nature of business operations, finance, marketing and human resources within a business context *and* How these interdependencies underpin business decision making

REVISED

This part of the specification is very different from the other parts because it is about the *links* that exist between the different business functions. There are four functions – business operations, finance, marketing and human resources – and you should already have studied and revised these. You need to know what these links are and how a business should consider them when making decisions. The examples below illustrate the **interdependent nature of business** and show some links between departments.

Interdependent nature of business: Refers to the links between different areas of business that affect decision making, the risks and rewards of business activity and the use of financial information to aid business decision making.

Example

Link

- Business operations (producing goods or services) and human resources (workers).
- The *amount* that a business produces and *how* a business produces will link with the number and type of workers it needs.

Decisions

- A gardening business may want to increase the number of customers it has. It is likely to need to increase the number of gardeners it employs, in order to carry out work for new customers.
- A firm manufactures and fits signs, including road signs and signs placed on or outside buildings. It wants to increase production. It may be able to do this by introducing new technology such as robots to carry out the manufacturing process. This may require more skilled specialists to control the technology. It may need to employ more fitters to fit the signs. It might be able to lay off some workers whose job can now be done by new technology.

Example

Link

- Business operations and finance.

Decisions

- A business wishes to expand production by building a new factory.
- The finance department will have to arrange finance for this, perhaps by selling shares or taking out a bank loan.

Example

Link

- Business operations and marketing.

Decisions

- A firm wishes to increase production.
- The marketing department may decide to increase advertising and other marketing activities to make sure the business can sell the increased output. It may also change its marketing, for example, advertising nationally rather than just locally.

Example

Link

- Finance and marketing.

Decisions

- A firm may want to increase its marketing to introduce a new product or because of increased competition.
- The finance department will have to finance this spending, perhaps by arranging an overdraft or finding the money in the business' reserves.

Now test yourself

TESTED

Merseyside Beds Ltd produces mattresses and bed frames in its Liverpool factory located just outside the city centre. The company wants to increase production and is considering building a new factory on a disused site on the outskirts of the city.

Analyse the possible effect on each of the following if Merseyside Beds increases production by building a new factory. [9]

1 Human resources
2 Finance
3 Marketing

I can ...

- ☐ Identify links between different business functions.
- ☐ Analyse how different business functions may be linked.

Exam tip

If you are asked a question about how a business decision might affect the different functions in a business, remember that there may be more than one way in which the decision affects each function.

Impact of risk and reward on business activity *and* Use of financial information in measuring and understanding business performance and decision making

REVISED

Businesses use **financial information** to help them make decisions. The information can help to maximise the profit a business can make and reduce its chances of making a loss. Business information may be either forecasts or records. Forecasts are predictions of what *may* happen. Records show what *did* happen but there are no guarantees that what did happen will continue to happen in the future. So, while business information is useful in making decisions, businesses must think about other things that can affect their decisions, for example:

- new competition entering a market which could affect sales, prices and expected revenues
- changes in costs, including wages, will be affected by the level of unemployment, while material costs will be affected by a world shortage or a change in the exchange rate of the pound.

When making decisions, businesses also need to consider the impact of **non-financial risk** and **non-financial rewards**. The examples below show how financial information can measure performance and help decision making.

Financial information: Includes information about revenues, costs, profit, rates of return, break-even and cash flow. Financial information helps a business to make decisions.

Non-financial rewards: To owners, this includes the satisfaction of running a successful business, being in charge, being independent and having an impact on what consumers buy.

Non-financial risk: To business owners, this includes their health due to stress and strained relationships with family and friends.

Example

Decision: Is the business making a good profit?

Profit figures may help with this judgement, but a better way to decide is to calculate the average rate of return (ARR), which gives owners a percentage rate of return on their investment. A business' ARR can be compared with that made by other businesses, or with how much they could earn in interest by saving their money. This can help a business decide whether its performance is good enough, if changes are needed to improve **business performance**, if it should switch its investment to a different line of business or simply save its money instead. (For more information, see Section 5.3, page 92.)

Business performance: A measure of how well a business is doing. Key measures are sales, profits and rates of return.

Example

Decision: Increasing sales revenue

A business may decide it needs to increase sales revenue to increase profits. Revenue can be increased by raising the price of what it sells or increasing the amount it sells. A rise in price usually leads to lower sales, although sales revenue may rise if sales do not fall very much. Financial information predicting the effects of changes in price will help the business to make this decision.

Example

Decision: Reducing costs

A business may decide to increase its profits by reducing costs, through the introduction of new technology. Using financial information, it could calculate the cost of buying and using the new technology and any savings that might result by reducing the amount of labour it employs. (For more information, see Section 5.3, pages 89–91.)

Example

Decision: Producing a new product

A business may want to produce a new product. Break-even analysis will help the business decide how many it must sell, and at what price, to make a profit. If the business does not think it can sell this amount, it may decide not to produce the new product so that it does not make a loss on it. Alternatively, it may look at ways of reducing the cost, or raising the price, to make the new product profitable. (For more information, see Section 5.4, pages 93–95.)

Example

Decision: How to finance business activities

A cash flow forecast may show that a business will have a negative cash flow for a time (see Section 5.5, page 96). The business may consider having an overdraft or using trade credit, if possible. From the cash flow forecast the business could find out how much finance it will need, and for how long. This information, and the interest rate it would be charged for the period, could be used to calculate the cost. (For more information, see Section 5.2, pages 83–84.)

Now test yourself

TESTED ☐

Jo Swindale runs a convenience store, which is open seven days a week from 7 a.m. until 6 p.m. She is considering keeping the shop open until 10 p.m. She would need to employ two additional workers to share the 6–10 p.m. shift during the week. Jo needs information to decide whether to open for the additional hours.

1 Explain how financial information would help Jo to make this decision. [6]

Supersmoothies Ltd makes smoothie drinks from fruit. The company is considering expanding by buying either a fruit grower in Spain or a fruit grower in Israel. Using information provided by the two fruit growers, the financial director of Supersmoothies has estimated that the average rate of return (ARR) from investing money in the Spanish company would be 8 per cent and 10.5 per cent from the Israeli business in the first year. Wage costs in Spain have been low and have not risen much in the past 10 years, although employment is expected to start to rise in the next year.

2 Explain the possible **financial risk** and **financial reward** to Supersmoothies Ltd in buying another business. [4]

3 Evaluate whether the information about the Spanish and Israeli businesses is useful to Supersmoothies in helping it to decide which business to buy. [7]

Exam tip

An exam question may give financial data. Be ready to recommend a decision based on the financial information given and, if the question directs you, any other information you consider to be relevant. Another type of question may ask you to state the financial information that a business needs to make a decision.

Financial reward: The profit made by business.

Financial risk: The possibility a business will lose money from decisions it makes. Owners may lose money they have invested.

I can ...

☐ State the financial information a business should use for different types of decisions.

☐ Analyse and evaluate financial information to make recommendations about business decisions.